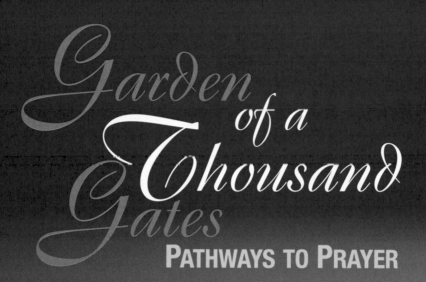

Garden of a Thousand Gates

of a

PATHWAYS TO PRAYER

Carl Koch and Contributors

Saint Mary's Press
Christian Brothers Publications
Winona, Minnesota

Contributors

Armand Alcazar, FSC
Janis Best
Rev. Steven Brice
Margaret Holcombe
Lynn Tooma, SSND

Genuine recycled paper with 10% post-consumer waste.
Printed with soy-based ink.

The publishing team included Carl Koch, series editor; Rosemary Broughton, development editor; Rebecca Fairbank, copy editor; Gary J. Boisvert, production editor, typesetter, and cover designer; Maurine R. Twait, art director; Evy Abrahamson, illustrator; David Noton, International Stock Photo, cover photographer; pre-press, printing, and binding by the graphics division of Saint Mary's Press.

The acknowledgments continue on page 186.

Printed in the United States of America

Printing: 9 8 7 6 5 4 3 2 1

Year: 2006 05 04 03 02 01 00 99 98

ISBN 0-88489-497-5

CONTENTS

Getting in Touch with Prayer

1. **What Is Prayer?**   *8*
2. **Where Do We Meet God?**   *22*
3. **Who Is the God We Encounter in Prayer?**   *32*

Ways of Praying

4. Petition:
   Asking God for Help   *48*
5. Thanks and Praise:
   Giving God a Joyful Heart   *62*
6. Journal Writing:
   A Conversation with God   *76*
7. Meditation:
   Dwelling on the Mystery of God   *92*
8. Praying with the Scriptures:
   Nourished by the Word   *110*
9. Community Prayer:
   Binding Us Together with God   *128*
10. The Eucharist:
    Celebrating Jesus' Saving Presence   *144*
11. Traditional Prayer:
    Praying Together in One Voice   *162*

Epilogue: Growing in a Life of Prayer   *180*

Getting in Touch with Prayer

1

WHAT IS PRAYER?

Throughout human history, and through all the centuries of the Christian tradition, women and men have been drawn to prayer. This book is an introduction to Christian prayer, an opportunity to learn about and to practice different forms of prayer. Our first consideration must be, What is prayer? To answer this question, we need to consider the fundamental human experience of the sacred.

Encountering the Sacred

Human beings have a strong, natural urge to reach out to something beyond themselves—to something they can sense but never capture. This urge is a way of seeking meaning and peace in their life. In this chapter we will explore the experience of reaching beyond ourselves—of meeting with mystery, with the sacred. We will see that this experience can occur and be described in many different ways. And we will see that the encounter with the sacred is at the heart of the Christian understanding of prayer in any form.

Stories of Common Human Experience

It is reasonable to wonder: What does my life have to do with the sacred? Is it really something I can experience? Keeping up with commitments, relationships, and decisions about the future might seem like more than enough to do without looking for the sacred. But common human experience—our private and shared lives—is filled with possibilities for encountering the sacred. The following stories provide examples of such meetings in various avenues of life. Perhaps one or more of them will have elements that are familiar to you.

In Nature and Solitude

Many people find a sense of the sacred when they are in situations that bring them close to nature. For Hannah, a young professional woman, the natural world sparked a welcome experience when she least expected it—on a ski trip to Colorado for her winter vacation. When her friends welcomed her home, she told them this story:

> The slopes were so crowded that the skiing wasn't enjoyable. One day I'd had enough, so I went for a walk by myself. Pretty soon I was out of town on a trail. It was totally deserted. At first I was a little afraid, but then I began to enjoy the silence. It was a steep climb, so after a bit I stopped to catch my breath. I sat on a rock and looked around. I was only a little way from the ski village, but it was absolutely quiet. The way the sun hit the snow, it sparkled like a million diamonds. And a grove of trees in front of me looked so deep and black, like midnight. For some reason all of a sudden I knew that God was right there. I felt it—just like someone was standing next to me. I sat there for

the longest time, just letting myself feel the peace and love. It may sound strange, but it was an incredible experience.

Jason is a busy high school teacher in a big city. He coaches basketball for the school team and plays in a YMCA league. He volunteers part-time at an inner-city soup kitchen, and he has recently become engaged. Jason often finds that solitude provides much-needed refreshment from his hectic lifestyle. When he needs to get away from it all, he goes by himself up to the roof of his apartment building. He comments:

> I sit there and listen to the sounds from the street twelve floors down. It all seems so far away then. And I think about Anne and our future together, the challenges of school and the students I am with each day, but once in a while I notice I am not thinking about anything, I just feel peaceful and content.

Through Special People

Sometimes a sense of the sacred may come to us through the personality of someone who is special to us or whose special qualities seem to spread out toward others. One such person was Rosie, who is remembered in this account from a man she once baby-sat:

> Rosie's husband died young. Her oldest son died of cancer. Her granddaughter died of cancer. Her youngest son has bravely combated cancer all his life. When Rosie was in her early twenties, one of her breasts was removed. . . .
>
> . . . Her kitchen was lit for the night with a small, single bulb which gave the room a soft, inside-of-a-pumpkin glow. In the bottom right-hand drawer of her cabinet Rosie had every type of candy: Three Musketeers, Milky Ways, Turkish Taffy, M&M's. I would not have been surprised if the roof and shingles of Rosie's house had been made of gingerbread. . . .
>
> Rosie liked to sit in her side porch and have you sit beside her. She liked to talk about New York City and what it was like when she was a girl: the parrot the trolley conductor kept on his shoulder, the sinking of a ferryboat

which killed many church-picnic goers and how she couldn't go that morning because she had diphtheria. Rosie liked to talk about the convict she had helped, about gathering horse manure for the garden, about her famous bridge games over at the firehouse. Her stories were just as good as the *Arabian Nights.*

There are perhaps fifty people who even knew that Rosie ever existed. Perhaps you have a Rosie down your street, across from you in your building, or deep in your memory. . . .

I owe much of my imagination to Rosie, because she was nearly too good to be real. (Christopher de Vinck, *Only the Heart Knows How to Find Them,* pages 58–60)

Another special person was Andy, who ran a diner in New Jersey. He had a gift for making people feel that they mattered.

Andy was a good man. Many poor people traveled by bus from Newark to the many factories in the area. It was not unusual for some of them to stop into the diner and ask Andy for food or money.

> **The sacred may come to us through the personality of someone special.**

He was softhearted. After a lecture on the meager state of his own resources, Andy would ask Jack [the cook] to prepare a take-out breakfast and would place a five-dollar bill on the little tray before Jack wrapped it up. Those people were often forlorn, forgotten, lonely. They needed someplace where their lives could be given value simply because their stories and troubles were listened to. (Jeff Behrens, "Andy's Diner," in Gregory F. Augustine Pierce, editor, *Of Human Hands,* page 32)

◆ Recall a person you have known whose special qualities could be said to convey a sense of the sacred.

Through the Mystery of Life and Death

Death is an important reality of human existence that concerns us all. But it is a reality that we can never fully understand, so we consider it a mystery. If we reflect on the mystery of life and death, we may see many instances of a sense of the sacred coming through. For example, Alexander's mother died when he was only twelve. Now he is married with three teenage children and is making plans for their college education. Since his mother's death, the changing seasons have become more significant to him.

> Sometimes I feel depressed in the winter, when the trees are bare and everything is gray. And that's when I remember my mother's death the most. But when the first signs of spring start to show, I become grateful for the gift of life. It reminds me that my mother is still alive in who I am and in my family.

Something similar happened among the parish staff at a suburban Catholic church who lost a dear friend and coworker in the religious education director, Leah. After a difficult struggle with bone marrow cancer, Leah died just before the students' confirmation day. Throughout her six-month illness, the parish staff and the students in this confirmation class came together with a spirit they had never before experienced at their parish. Not only did they raise money for Leah's medical bills, but they put on a talent show to cheer her up, and made her laugh so hard that she felt better than she had in months.

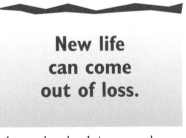

New life can come out of loss.

Many of the students, even those who had been wary of being around serious illness and suffering, spent hours at Leah's bedside keeping her company. One student said:

> It's kind of amazing, you know. I'd never been around anyone that was dying before, and I was spooked about it at first. But after a few times visiting her, it didn't seem uncomfortable. We would just talk and talk about things I

never say to other people. I felt like a new person around her. With her, maybe because she was dying, the rules about what to talk about seemed different. It was so awful when she finally died; I just couldn't believe she was gone. But I look back on those visits as very special times, some of the happiest I can ever remember, even though it makes me cry to think of them.

What Is Happening in These Stories?

What do all these accounts have to do with prayer? What do they all have in common? Each of them describes a simple human behavior—walking, grieving, talking—and an encounter with something beyond ordinary, everyday human activities. The people in these stories have confronted the possibility that there are multiple dimensions in life as we live it day by day.

People use all kinds of words to describe their experiences. Those words all try to explain a reality that is beyond the visible, physical phenomenon, a reality that fills people with awe. They point us to a mystery or a divine presence that is at the heart of human experience.

Your Life Story

Think for a moment about your own personal story. What has been the most positive moment of your life so far? Was it an experience that you planned for, or did it creep up on you unexpectedly? Have you ever gotten out of bed in the morning with the feeling that it was going to be a wonderful day and had that feeling reinforced by everything that happened to you? For most of us, the good moments dominate our life. If we open our senses, we find the sacred all around us, in simple things like a rosebud just opening, or the pattern of the bricks on the side of an old building, or the love of a spouse, children, relatives, coworkers, and friends. Sometimes we experience sacred moments in the midst of a great adventure, but most often we find them in the little things of life that we can easily take for granted.

Think, too, about some of your more difficult times. Like Leah's students and coworkers, and Kevin, who experienced the death of his mother at a young age, have you had a difficult or painful experience that made you ask, Why did this have to happen? Sometimes questions like this have no easy answers. But after such experiences we do have to go on. We keep living in the hope that we'll get beyond the pain and grief to new understanding. And often we find that we have learned and grown a great deal through it all. Difficult experiences show us that it is possible to experience sacred moments even in the midst of great grief or suffering.

The Christian Experience of the Sacred

A Variety of Religious Traditions

Encounters with the sacred take on a special meaning when they occur in the context of one's religious tradition. Human beings naturally try to find meaning in life and look beyond the ordinary to find it. This aspect of human nature has led to the development of a great variety of religious traditions around the world.

Each tradition has been marked and given its character by unique circumstances. For instance, the climate and terrain of a particular region can strongly influence the way its residents give expression to their encounter with the sacred in nature. People who live in a dry, barren region may find the sacred in the rain that falls only occasionally. The sun can be a means of experiencing the sacred for those who rely on it for their livelihood and well-being. Also, a population's political and economic status can shape its religious tradition. An oppressed population will image and respond to the sacred differently than will the group that is oppressing it. In various cultures, a minority group may image the sacred differently than those who are considered mainstream. Whatever the specifics, in every known religious tradition, the encounter with the sacred is of central and deep importance.

Grace and the Paschal Mystery: Through Death to Life

As Christians we interpret our encounters with the sacred from the perspective of the Christian tradition. Encountering the sacred is, in Christian terms, an experience of grace. Grace is the loving and active presence of God in the world. An experience of grace is freely given by God in many ways, including one that has its direct origin in the story of the death and Resurrection of Jesus.

The Christian perspective has at its core the view that when Jesus died and rose from the dead, he gave us hope that death is not the end of everything. In the Christian way of understanding, the mystery of life and death focuses on the death and Resurrection of Jesus, and what we learn from reflecting on this mystery can greatly affect our life and our prayer.

When applied to Jesus, the mystery of life and death is called the paschal mystery. Jesus preached the gospel, then suffered and died, but on the third day he rose from the dead. Life triumphed over death. In our own life, evidence of the paschal mystery may not be quite so dramatic, but it is still significant. We all experience loss and sadness, perhaps in the death of a family member or friend, or in the loss of a relationship. Our response to these losses might be to give in to despair or to lose all hope. But if, during our hard times, we reflect on how our own life is part of the paschal mystery, Jesus' suffering, death, and Resurrection can offer us courage and hope.

It is easy to say the words "New life can come out of loss," but like any mystery, the paschal mystery is not always easy to perceive and understand, especially during difficult times. Nevertheless, Jesus himself put it directly when he said, "'Very truly, I tell you, unless a grain of wheat falls into the earth and dies, it remains just a single grain; but if it dies, it bears much fruit'" (John 12:24).

◆ Have you ever had a "death-to-life" experience through which you were able to grow because of something difficult you lived through?

What has been your most serious loss? What form did your grief take? What grace was given that altered your faith, hope, or love?

 What has been your greatest gain? What form did your joy take? How did this grace change your faith, hope, or love?

The Sacraments

In a general sense, the word *sacrament* refers to any sign of God's presence. Throughout this chapter we have looked at many experiences and moments that could be described as sacramental. And in the Catholic Tradition, certain special symbolic acts, like blessing oneself with holy water and saying the rosary, are even called sacramentals.

The Catholic church also specifies as sacraments seven particular ritual events through which it expresses faith and worship. These sacraments are baptism, confirmation, the Eucharist, reconciliation (or penance), anointing of the sick, marriage, and holy orders. The seven sacraments can be thought of as ritual celebrations of the paschal mystery. They are transformative events. In baptism, for example, we enter into a new life in Christ. In the Eucharist we share directly in the mystery of the death and Resurrection of Jesus. The paschal mystery is the transformative reality that is celebrated in the sacraments, and in our celebrations we make this reality visible.

Participating in the sacraments celebrates and underlines God's presence and action in our life. For example, when receiving the Eucharist, we are invited to sense God's presence in a much more immediate way than at other times of the day or week. Similarly, people who participate in the baptism of an infant often experience a sense of God's presence with this fragile new being. They find themselves understanding in a fresh way what it means to be part of the community of faith. The ritual becomes an opening into the sacred, into an awareness that all of life is blessed by the presence of God.

Other Life Experiences

We find ourselves touched by awe at many times other than just the official occasions of prayer and liturgy. These other events, too, can be understood from a Christian perspective and can enhance our experience of faith.

You may have experienced God as present to you during an unusual sunset when you were driving home from work, or when sitting alone in a quiet corner of your kitchen. You may have experienced God's presence when sharing with family or friends and deepening your relationships, or when those you love have been drawn together by the pain of a tragic event.

You may know God's presence when sharing with friends.

We might also experience God's presence in the thanks of a stranger or in the faces of people who are suffering. Such encounters may help give us a fresh new understanding of Jesus and his teachings in the Gospels. A young man encountering homelessness on his first trip to New York City said:

> It seemed like the parable of the good Samaritan was right in front of my eyes. Everyone was walking right past all these people who were suffering, and I didn't know how to respond. So I thought a lot about it, and then I got involved with the food pantry back home. It's a small thing, but I'm working on ways to do more.

Responding to the Sacred

When the people introduced in this chapter encountered the sacred, most of them responded in a positive fashion—they appreciated the value of their experience and developed themselves through it. There are, however, other ways to respond, and each of us may react in different ways at different times.

Rationalization

At times we might reject any suggestion that the sacred exists. During these times, we view things at a literal level. If we encounter questions or mystery, we rationalize it, or make it seem reasonable, by saying it could be explained logically if only we had enough data. We might also choose to ignore an encounter with mystery, and this is in itself a kind of response. For the times when we do not want to acknowledge our experience, we can usually find plenty of ways to explain away the unexplainable.

Ridicule

It is often easier to ridicule things we do not understand than to work toward comprehending them. We commonly make jokes to cover up fears and uncertainties. Sometimes we arrogantly dismiss or make fun of important issues in order to avoid seeking answers to difficult questions.

Faith

Responding to the sacred with faith involves trust and courage. We trust that a particular situation or experience is given to us as an opportunity for growth and learning, and our trust is in God, who is the source of the opportunity. It takes courage to recognize that life involves more than can be explained by everyday reality. It takes courage to accept tough experiences because we trust that something good will come from them. So responding to the sacred with faith means accepting courageously our given circumstances because we trust God, the source of life and all its conditions.

The response of faith goes even further. Having trusted God, we recognize more and more the activity of God. Faith opens us to the experience of sacred moments and enables us to respond to that presence of God with us. But how can we maintain this kind of dynamic relationship with a God we cannot see or touch? That is where prayer comes in.

How Does Prayer Fit In?

We have been speaking about encountering the sacred in various aspects of our life. We have looked at different responses to these encounters. Prayer fits in throughout this whole process, as we can see if we consider this basic definition:

Prayer is awareness of God and response to the presence of the sacred in all our life.

This definition may not be quite what you expected. It does not identify prayer as certain words spoken or thought at certain times. Rather, it presents prayer as awareness (knowledge) of God's presence and response (reaction) to that presence.

Br. David Steindl-Rast, a writer and teacher of spirituality, says, "We must distinguish prayer from prayers" (*Gratefulness, the Heart of Prayer,* page 211). This does not mean that prayers are not important. They are. But consider this phrase from our definition of prayer: "in all our life." Most of us cannot constantly be saying prayers. Steindl-Rast goes on to say: "Saying prayers is one activity among others. But prayer is an attitude of the heart that can transform every activity" (page 211). So prayer consists of being aware of God's presence and responding to it. Naturally we are not going to be consciously aware of God all the time, because we are limited human beings. The awareness of God that is characteristic of a prayerful person is at a deeper, more attitudinal level than a conscious level.

If we reflect on this, we may feel that we are not adequately involved in prayer. We may sense that we are not fully aware of, or do not respond well to, God's presence, and that may be so. But when we reach beyond ourselves in an attempt to find meaning and peace, we are praying. As Steindl-Rast puts it, "Moments in which we drink deeply from the source of meaning are moments of prayer, whether we call them so or not" (page 211). Prayerful living happens in anyone who seeks to live a meaningful life. By living with a searching heart, we are recognizing and responding to God's presence.

◆ Think of a personal experience that you have not before thought of as prayer but that seems to be included in the wider notion of prayer discussed here.

Where Do We Go from Here?

We Ask *Who, What, Where, When, Why*

Reading this book is a journey in which we hope to enrich our prayer life. In part A, chapters 1 to 3, we are building a foundation for this by trying to answer some questions. In this chapter we have formulated a basic definition to answer the question *What* is prayer? We have also considered *why* we pray—to respond to God's presence. And we have discovered *when* we can pray—in all the moments of our life.

In the next chapter, we will consider the question *Where* do we meet God? We will see that God is present in all our relationships. We will explore ways we respond to that sacred presence in our relationships with ourselves, with others, and with the universe God has created.

In chapter 3 we will ask, *Who* is this God we encounter in prayer? We will consider the many ways God has been understood and imaged in the Scriptures and tradition. We will also reflect on the ways that we learn about God through our own experiences.

We Ask *How*

With the foundation for study and reflection given in the first part of the book, part B will then explore the *how* of praying, some practical methods for our prayer life, in both its personal and public forms.

In chapters 4 to 8 we will explore several ways of enriching our personal prayer life: petition, thanks and praise, journal writing, meditation, and praying with the Scriptures.

Personal prayer is the starting point for public prayer, or prayer in community. In chapters 9 to 11 we will look at community prayer services as well as the Eucharist. We will also spend some time considering traditional prayers, seeing if we can rediscover meaning in them for ourselves.

Through all this exploration, our goal is to grow in our life of prayer by deepening our understanding and acquiring new methods that we can use to help us be aware of God's presence in all that we do.

◆ Throughout this book you will encounter reflection activities. These invite you to spend some time getting involved in a subject or a form of prayer and meditation. These activities can enrich your experience significantly.

2

WHERE DO WE MEET GOD?

Where do we encounter the sacred? Where do we meet God?

These are important questions. After all, in the Gospel of John we are told, "No one has ever seen God" (1:18). But although we cannot "see" God, we encounter the sacred in many ways, even when we do not recognize it. Three areas in which we can experience the sacred are self, others, and creation.

Encountering God in Self

To take a picture, a photographer needs a camera. The camera is a complex tool that allows the photographer to perceive, to encounter, to meet the world in a particular way. The most important part of the camera is the lens. Without the lens, the subject in front of the camera cannot be brought into focus; it cannot be composed in a special way; and it cannot be transferred to the camera's memory, the film. In other words the lens provides the necessary element for the camera to function as a camera.

In a similar way, human beings cannot function as human beings without the lens called the self. All that we understand—about ourselves, those around us, and the world at large—is perceived and interpreted through the self. Like a camera lens, the self is hard to describe, and when it works best it is unseen.

Try to think of a time that you felt a strong sense of contentment—a time that you were at peace, no matter how briefly. Perhaps it was during a quiet break from a hectic workday, or maybe it was while embracing someone you care deeply about, or possibly it was in the still moments following an outbreak of heartfelt laughter. Such a feeling can be thought of as an experience of the self in a pure moment, when the self is not obstructed by insecurity or vanity, or by desires for certain things. It is like the moment when a perfect photograph is about to be taken—when everything is in place, the camera is all set, and the light is just right.

Being Created in the Image of God

The self is at the heart of all that we encounter, so when we try to answer the question Where do we meet God? we must begin with ourselves. This is also a quite natural place to begin because human beings have a unique relationship with God, as shown in the Creation stories.

The Book of Genesis begins with stories of the creation of the world. These stories offer a poetic vision of the order of Creation. With earth, water, plants, and animals in their place, it came time to bring human beings into the world:

> So God created humankind in his image,
> in the image of God he created them;
> male and female he created them.
>
> (Genesis 1:27)

As God's representatives, we human beings are meant to participate actively with God in all that we do.

In the Genesis story, human beings are images of God before they have language, relationships, art, science, or even personality. In comparison think of a newborn human baby. At first a particular infant seems just like any other infant, but soon she begins to develop her own distinctive characteristics—the way she grabs her toes or curls her fingers next to her cheek, the particular voice of her cry. Because of her natural curiosity about herself, she quickly becomes more than just a baby like any other baby. She is separate and distinct and recognizable as an individual. Still, she is also recognizable as a human baby. She has not lost her original identity.

In a similar way, we maintain our identity as being made in the image of God. But as we grow and change, and identify ourselves in terms of human ideas, creations, and desires, we often lose sight of our basic identity as an image of God.

Acquiring Self-Knowledge

The quality of our self-knowledge determines the healthiness of our life in many respects, from our physical well-being to our relationship with God. All of us search to know who we are. The infant touching her toes is seeking self-knowledge, as is the troubled person who talks things over with a therapist or counselor. Self-knowledge can be influenced both positively and negatively by our experience. We learn about ourselves in many different ways and may encounter obstacles in the process. We see pitfalls as well as opportunities. Often just when we think we know ourselves fully, we have a new experience that reveals an aspect of our personality that we were not previously aware of. We should always keep in mind that the activity of gaining self-knowledge is challenging—but like most challenges, it has its rewards.

Hiding from Our Real Self

One obstacle to self-knowledge is the temptation to hide from our real self. Most of us can think of times when we have kept something about our self hidden—maybe even from ourselves as well as others. For example, Lauren enjoyed a different style of music than most of her friends. But rather than set herself apart by this difference, she hid it from her peers. In the process she also hid it more and more from herself, until she lost it.

We often keep our real self hidden like this because of fear. The concern that others will know us for who we really arc also prevents us from fully knowing and loving ourselves. This anxiety can be quite real—we may be afraid that people will use this knowledge against us or that we will bc humiliated and rejected. Fear can keep us from looking within to discover the person we really are.

At first it is as though we have a picket fence hiding us. Glimpses of our real self can be seen through the spaces from time to time. But as we cover up truths about ourselves or avoid facing problems in our life, we close up the openings in the fence. The fence becomes a wall, and we remain hidden. The more we cover up parts of who we truly are, the less our genuine self can be known and accepted. We may reach the point where even we no longer recognize our true self. Part of growing in self-knowledge is accepting who we are and letting that real self out from behind the fences and walls that hide us.

Getting Stuck in the Negative

Another obstacle to self-knowledge is the tendency to get stuck in the negative. Somewhere along the line we may have gotten the idea that life is supposed to be a disagreeable experience. We may have been tempted to think that God loves us more when we are sad and lonely than when we are happy and connected. Of course God loves people who suffer, but God's love is freely given to all. We sometimes forget that the negative aspects of our life are normal and that we need these experiences to help us grow in a positive fashion. However, getting stuck in negative ways of thought and expression blocks us from recognizing our identity as an image of God. It inhibits our participation in the life of God, who is love. We must be alert to the temptation to diminish ourselves by denying God's life within us.

You may remember experiences when you kept a part of yourself in hiding, or when you focused too much on the negative aspects of your life.

◆ How did these experiences restrict you from being an effective representative of the love of God?
◆ What might you do in the future to keep your true self open to yourself and others?

Reflecting on Oneself with God

To increase our self-knowledge, we can reflect on what we know about ourselves, actually talk to ourselves about who we are and who we want to be. For example, one person wrote about a conflict with some friends: "I sure reacted vehemently when I found out that

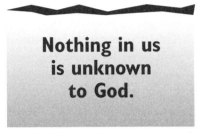

Nothing in us is unknown to God.

they went to the theater without inviting me. I was angry, but mostly my pride was wounded. I guess I'm more frightened about being excluded than I thought." This kind of self-talk is a way of maintaining a relationship with ourselves. That relationship can be good or bad; it can help us to grow and be healthy, or it can hinder us. Our goal is to develop a positive, constructive relationship. This person's self-talk is leading in that direction because it is honest about difficult feelings and accepting of them.

Meeting God in Self-Reflection

When we practice self-reflection prayerfully, we recognize God's presence in our relationship with ourselves. With God present in this encounter, this relationship naturally becomes a positive one. Nothing can be hidden when God is part of our self-reflection. God knows about all the hidden places within us, all the elements of our inner being that we think we can never share with another person. We cannot hide behind our fence of fear when we meet God prayerfully in self-reflection. When we reflect on our self with God, we reflect on the sacred mystery of our own being. This real and sacred self is the self we want to come to know in reflection.

Bringing Our Whole Self to Prayer

One aspect of prayer is the willingness to open up fully to God, who knows our real self and who, knowing everything about us, loves us freely and fully. We may or may not love ourselves fully, but because of God's freely given love we always have the ability and opportunity to bring our whole self to God in prayer. God loves us the way we are, so with God we do not have to pretend to be at ease or confident, fearless or perfect. We can celebrate our joys, accomplishments, and talents because God celebrates with us. Or we can ache over our sorrows, defeats, and fears because God longs to restore our wholeness.

The more we learn to love ourselves for who we really are, the more we have to offer others and God. Self-reflection in the loving presence of God, which is prayer, enables us to give fully of ourselves in our relationships with God and others.

Encountering God in Others

Individual people exist in community with others, and so it is that we must turn to others to discover more fully where we meet God.

The Scriptures tell us that our relationship with others is the true indicator of our relationship with God. As Saint John says, "Those who say, 'I love God,' and hate their brothers or sisters, are liars; for those who do not love a brother or sister whom they have seen, cannot love God whom they have not seen" (1 John 4:20).

The Body of Christ

The community of God's people can be referred to in Christian terms as the Body of Christ. In his writings, Saint Paul used the image of the Body of Christ to help the Christians in Rome understand that although they were individuals, they were also parts of one united community:

> In one body we have many members, and not all the members have the same function, so we, who are many, are one body in Christ, and individually we are members one of another. (Romans 12:4–5)

Unity in Diversity

A necessary element of the Body of Christ is diversity. Similarly, all the members of a community have different skills and gifts, and they all depend on one another. A community cannot function in a healthy manner without diversity and cooperation.

If the coach of a baseball team sent nine very good pitchers onto the field together. Chances are they would not perform well as a team because their skills are not diverse. The talent of a pitcher and the talents of a catcher and fielders are interdependent. These diverse abilities unite in a team that can perform well. It is the same in any community. The community members function in diverse ways but are united—their larger goal is the same.

Seeing with Eyes of Faith

Saint Paul, in his First Letter to the Corinthians, remarks:

> Now there are varieties of gifts, but the same Spirit; and there are varieties of services, but the same Lord; and there are varieties of activities, but it is the same God who activates all of them in everyone. To each is given the manifestation of the Spirit for the common good. (12:4–7)

To experience what Paul is speaking of, we might need to open our eyes in a new way, to see others—strangers as well as people that we know—through eyes of faith. This means seeing prayerfully; seeing with our heart; seeing others, as best we can, the way God sees them. Seeing others in this way, we may begin to understand God's love for each of us and to appreciate the wonderful variety of gifts God gives to the Body of Christ.

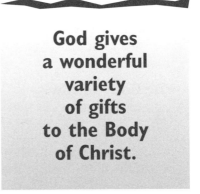

God gives a wonderful variety of gifts to the Body of Christ.

Saint Paul was seeing with eyes of faith when he wrote to the Christians at Galatia:

> There is no longer Jew or Greek, there is no longer slave or free, there is no longer male and female; for all of you are one in Christ Jesus. (Galatians 3:28)

Seeing others with eyes of faith is one step in learning to value people for who they really are. It is also a way to overcome prejudice and a way to better understand those we consider our enemies. When we meet God in others, or recognize others as the image of God, we make great strides toward building up the Body of Christ on earth.

Reread the passages from the writings of Paul quoted in Romans 12:4–5, I Corinthians 12:4–7, and Galatians 3:28.
◆ Think of some analogies that help illustrate the idea of the Body of Christ.
◆ Recall some of the gifts, services, and activities that you see in people you encounter in everyday life—family members, co-workers, friends, and strangers.
◆ How do those gifts, services, and activities add to the good of the whole community?
◆ Consider someone you do not like, or who "rubs you the wrong way." Try to see that person prayerfully, with eyes of faith.

People Who Are Poor and Oppressed

It is relatively easy to understand the idea of meeting God in our friends and loved ones. It may be more difficult to think of meeting God in the many people all over the world who are poor and oppressed, not part of our daily concerns. They may seem very remote to us. But the Christian Scriptures proclaim that this is exactly where we most need to meet God in others. Jesus clearly identifies his ministry with the poor and oppressed. The Spirit of God, he says, "'has anointed me to bring good news to the poor'" (Luke 4:18). It is necessary that we meet God in all to whom Jesus brought Good News, even when they are remote from us.

Reflect further on meeting God in poor and oppressed people by reading Matthew 25:31–46. In this passage, Jesus identifies himself with those who are poor and suffering. He sees our actions, good and bad, regarding the poor and suffering as actions done to him: "'"Truly I tell you, just as you did it to one of the least of these who are members of my family, you did it to me"'" (verse 40).
◆ What does the passage from Matthew say about our need to meet God in others, especially in those who are not as fortunate as we are?
◆ If everyone believed in the message of this passage, what changes might we see in society?

Encountering God in Creation

Henry Ward Beecher, the nineteenth-century American clergyman, said, "Every artist dips his brush in his own soul, and paints his own nature into his pictures." For instance, when we view the *Mona Lisa,* we cannot help but encounter the painter, Leonardo da Vinci. Or when we look at a piece of American Indian sculpture, we encounter the person who carved it, even though we know nothing about him or her. Some sense of the artist's identity remains in what the artist has created.

It is similar with God and God's creation. Having made the world and humanity, God did not disappear. But just as we are not usually aware that we are encountering God in self and others, we are also often not able to see the presence of God in creation. You may be able to think of examples of this blocked perception, and you may have some ideas about why obstacles exist. At the heart of the matter, though, is a way of thinking that separates God, who is not visible, from creation, which is visible.

God and Creation in the Scriptures

In the Bible God is the source of creation, but also God continues to stay involved in what has been created. God is not like an author of a play who watches its performance from a distant balcony. The writers of the Scriptures perceived God as alive within creation. It is God the Creator who gives and sustains life, and it is to God that all of creation gives thanks and praise. Separating God from creation was far from the thoughts of the biblical authors.

The Psalms provide many expressions of the encounter with God in creation. In Psalm 65, for example, the Psalmist views creation in the light of God's presence:

> You are the hope of all the ends of the earth
>   and of the farthest seas.

(Verse 5)

The Psalmist is familiar with God's activity in the world. God is the source of sustenance for the earth and all, including humans, that live on it:

> You visit the earth and water it,
>   you greatly enrich it;
> the river of God is full of water;
>   you provide the people with grain,
>   for so you have prepared it.
> You water its furrows abundantly,
>   settling its ridges,
> softening it with showers,
>   and blessing its growth.
>
> (Verses 9–10)

The Psalmist has no doubt that God's presence in creation is right and good. In the final lines of the psalm, the pastures, hills, meadows, and valleys "shout and sing together for joy" (verse 13). The earth itself praises the Creator, who is present in all that God has made.

Honoring God in Creation

The writer of Psalm 65 would probably agree that if we violate creation, we violate God as well. When we honor and respect creation, on the other hand, we also bring those reactions to God. Recall that self-reflection can be a form of prayer, and that seeing others with eyes of faith is a way of approaching our relationships prayerfully. In a similar way, our actions and attitudes toward creation can be prayerful, mindful of God's presence there. They can enrich ourselves and the world. But without reflection and prayerfulness, our actions and attitudes toward the earth can be harmful and destructive.

Read all of Psalm 65, and look through your Bible for other examples of psalms that express the presence of God in creation.
- How do human attempts to assume "ownership" of creation stand in the way of our encounter with God in creation?
- In what ways have you encountered God in creation?

3

WHO IS THE GOD WE ENCOUNTER IN PRAYER?

In prayer we meet with God and respond to God's sacred presence. But who is this God we encounter? How do we think about and picture God, especially when God cannot be seen?

Every person who considers questions like these is likely to have a unique answer. The nature of God is ultimately a mystery; human beings can never fully "know" God. So our understanding of God depends very much on who we are, how we see the world and our relationships, and especially how we experience love.

Metaphors and Images

Metaphor is an important tool that we have developed for helping us talk about the world. For example, if we say, "The new baby was showered with affection," we are using metaphorical language. The baby was not being literally showered or rained on; he was receiving great amounts of affection from those who love him. Similarly, when we say that a computer has a memory, we are not saying that it has memories like our own—remembrances of growing up, of good times, and so on. We are saying that the computer can store information, which is somewhat like having a human memory.

Metaphor helps us talk about the world, and we also need it in order to talk about God. Metaphorical language about God abounds in the Scriptures, in the Christian tradition, and in our everyday conversation. Jesus himself used many metaphors to describe his relationship with God, and more have developed as people have explored their connection with God throughout the centuries.

These metaphors provide us with images of God. For example, when Jesus said, "'I am the true vine, and my Father is the vinegrower'" (John 15:1), he was offering an image of God as one who lovingly plants, cares for, and harvests a crop that will provide refreshment and nourishment. Images of God help us to understand God more fully. Just as our human relationships are influenced by our impressions of others, so our relationship with God in prayer is influenced by our images of God.

The Limits of Images

Many images have been used to describe God because every image has limitations. Human language about God can never give a full picture of God. When we make an image of God for ourselves, it is necessarily based on our own experience, understanding, and imagination. No two people are exactly the same, nor are any two cultures, so the images we form of God will vary from person to person and culture to culture.

Once we have accepted that our images of God are always incomplete, we should examine these images to determine whether they help or hinder our relationship with God. Some images will draw us into our prayerful relationship with God, whereas others will seem to stand in the way. For instance, an image of God as a harsh judge may prevent us from being open with God in prayer. This image may make us fearful and reluctant to be "seen" by God as we are.

We may even find that different images are more effective at different times. If we are feeling hurt owing to a failed relationship with someone, an image of God as a provider of comfort may draw us into prayer. But if we are faced with a tough decision, God as the source of strength may be the image that helps us.

The Trinity

The image of the Trinity is a starting point for developing images of God. The Trinity is ultimately a mystery that can never be fully understood, but seeing God as Trinity means identifying three divine persons in one God. Traditionally the three persons are called the Father, the Son, and the Holy Spirit. Each person of the Trinity can be thought of as reflecting a particular relational aspect of the one God.

It is often said that God is love. The Scriptures teach this, especially in the words of John: "God is love, and those who abide in love abide in God, and God abides in them" (1 John 4:16). If God is love, then each person of the Trinity must have something to do with this love.

A typical human love relationship looks something like this:
- One person reaches out to another in love.
- One person receives that love and offers love in return.
- The love that is shared by the two persons has, in a way, a life of its own. It adds a new dimension to their lives and can even be "felt" by others.

The Trinity is much like this human relationship:
- God in the person of the Father is the lover, who reaches out, offering unconditional love.
- Jesus, the Son, is the beloved. He receives the love of the Father and, by embodying it, offers it back to the Father.

- The Holy Spirit is the shared love of the Father and the Son. Its influence is so strong that it adds a third person to this relationship, or community, of love.

  The dynamic of trinitarian love is not restricted to God in the image of Father, Son, and Holy Spirit. Some Christians call the three persons Creator, Redeemer, and Sustainer. The aspects of the Trinity—Lover, Beloved, and Shared Love—can be imaged in many ways.

◆ Apply the dynamics of love seen in the Trinity to your relationships with family and friends. Do new images of God come to mind? Do they enable you to see God in a new light, with a deeper understanding?

Enhancing Our Images of God the Father

Our images of God, being limited and imperfect, always need developing. A great variety of images of God can be found in the Scriptures. The richness of these images can add much to our prayer and help us to experience God more fully in the world.

Images of God in the Scriptures

When reading the Scriptures, try to be attentive to images of God that appear in the writings. Jot down images that are new to you. This will help you find the images that offer you the most meaningful experience of God.

"I Am"

In the Book of Exodus, when the Israelites are enslaved in Egypt, God sends Moses to liberate them. Moses asks God to give him an answer to the question he knows the Israelites will ask: "'What is [God's] name?'" (3:13). "God [says] to Moses, 'I AM WHO I AM.' [God says] further, 'Thus you shall say to the Israelites, "I AM has sent me to you"'" (verse 14).

"I AM" offers an image of God as the fullness of life. But this is not a passive image. God as "I AM" sends Moses, and calls and leads the people out of slavery. "I AM" is fullness, which is an active and freeing presence for the people.

All-Powerful God

God is considered to be omnipotent, or all-powerful. Such an image could be threatening and unsettling, but if we understand the will of God as a positive force, then an image of an all-powerful God can be quite liberating. In the biblical story of Job, after he has suffered great losses, Job recognizes that God has control over all things. He addresses God in this way:

"I know that you can do all things,
and that no purpose of yours can be thwarted."

(Job 42:2)

The image of God as all-powerful can be a great source of strength when we are feeling weak. Steadfast love is the foundation of God's love (Psalm 103:11), and by God's loving power all is created and given purpose:

He made my mouth like a sharp sword,
    in the shadow of his hand he hid me;
he made me a polished arrow,
    in his quiver he hid me away.

(Isaiah 49:2)

Another aspect of the image of God as omnipotent is God's sharing of power with humanity. The First Letter of Peter shows that God's power enables women and men to speak and serve:

Whoever speaks must do so as one speaking the very words of God; whoever serves must do so with the strength that God supplies, so that God may be glorified in all things through Jesus Christ. (4:11)

Imaging God's power as part of our prayer can help us to understand God's actions, because we derive our power from God.

God as Light and Guide

The image of God as light is seen in several places in the Scriptures, and it is easy to see why. In pitch darkness we are likely to feel vulnerable and helpless, and even a small glimmer of light makes a difference. The prophet Isaiah was acknowledging the presence of God as light when he described the experience of the people of Israel in this way:

The people who walked in darkness
    have seen a great light;
those who lived in a land of deep darkness—
    on them light has shined.

                        (Isaiah 9:2)

This image leads us to see God as our guide and teacher: "You guide me with your counsel" (Psalm 73:24). According to another psalm, God says,

I will instruct you and teach you the way you should go;
    I will counsel you with my eye upon you.

                       (Psalm 32:8)

In prayer we can call on God in the image of light and guide to help us discern our way or to help us with important decisions.

◆ Recall a time when you were "in the dark," lacking information or insight or wisdom that you needed in order to figure out what to do. Did you pray to God as light in that situation so that you could see your way more clearly?

Feminine Images of God

The masculine image of Father is often used in referring to God as the source of everything, but the Scriptures often describe God using feminine metaphors as well. God is neither male nor female, but in our human way of speaking of a personal God, we often think of God in terms of gender. In the Book of Isaiah, Israel is addressed by God imaged as a woman:

In the darkness, even the smallest light makes a difference.

As a mother comforts her child,
    so I will comfort you;
    you shall be comforted in Jerusalem.

                       (66:13)

In the Psalms, God is seen as a midwife assisting in the birth of a child:

> Yet it was you who took me from the womb;
> > you kept me safe on my mother's breast.
>
> > > (22:9)

Jesus, in this parable, also likens God to a woman:

> "Or what woman having ten silver coins, if she loses one of them, does not light a lamp, sweep the house, and search carefully until she finds it? When she has found it, she calls together her friends and neighbors, saying, 'Rejoice with me, for I have found the coin that I had lost.' Just so, I tell you, there is joy in the presence of the angels of God over one sinner who repents." (Luke 15:8–10)

In these examples God is imaged with human qualities that are traditionally associated with women: God is mother, midwife, and caretaker of the household. She comforts her children and keeps them safe; she cares for and rejoices over that which is precious to her.

God as Shepherd

The image of God as shepherd is frequently used in prayer and had great importance for the people of Israel. Sheep were a source of livelihood for many Israelites. Good, skilled shepherds were valued because of the care needed to successfully maintain a flock. Imaging God as a shepherd comforted people when they felt vulnerable, ignorant, or inadequate. Psalm 23 is probably the most famous example of the shepherd image, but Isaiah also used the metaphor: "[God] will feed his flock like a shepherd; / he will gather the lambs in his arms" (Isaiah 40:11).

◆ The image of God as shepherd may have less meaning today, when most of us have little experience of sheep and even less of shepherding. What might be a comparable image for God today?

God as *Abba*

In the Garden of Gethsemane, Jesus knew that he would soon be betrayed and would face death. Mark's Gospel describes Jesus at this time as "distressed and agitated" (14:33); he told his disciples, "'I am deeply grieved'" (verse 34). In this highly emotional state, Jesus prayed: "'Abba, Father, for you all things are possible; remove this cup from me; yet, not what I want, but what you want'" (verse 36).

The Aramaic word *abba* is an intimate term for "father." In English we would say "daddy" or "papa." Jesus repeatedly spoke of God as his Father, and experienced himself as God's Son. It is significant that in the depths of grief and distress, Jesus chose to address his prayer to God not simply as Father but as Daddy. Such an image of God the Father is tender, intimate, and accessible.

Saint Paul also used *abba* when he said that Christians have become like children again, and in their heart Jesus cries out, "Abba!" (see Galatians 4:6). This image suggests that God is a parent whom we can approach without fear, certain that we will be loved and accepted, even in our most painful and vulnerable moments.

Reflecting on Images of God

If we take some time to think about the numerous images of God, we are likely to be surprised at how many of them we recognize from our own experience and prayer.

◆ Look again at the images of God as "I am," all-powerful, light and guide, a woman, a shepherd, and *Abba.* Which ring true for you?

◆ What other images come to mind, from the Scriptures or any other source, that help you to better understand your life, the universe, and God's place in both?

Exploring Our Images of God the Son

The Second Person of the Trinity, traditionally referred to as the Son, or Word, became incarnate in the man Jesus, to manifest and embody the unifying love that is offered by God the Father.

Christians believe that Jesus is God incarnate—God made flesh as a human being.

Images of Jesus abound. These images are especially evident in the art that has been inspired by his life, death, and Resurrection. For nearly twenty centuries, sculptors and painters have depicted Jesus in all stages of his life—as an infant, as a young boy and man, dying on the cross, and resurrected. Artists have shown Jesus praying, eating meals, teaching, healing, driving merchants from the Temple, and so on. Representations of Jesus reflect the various cultures of the world. He has been portrayed with the features of many ethnic groups, including African, Mediterranean, Asian, Hispanic, and American Indian. Jesus speaks to all people in all cultures in all times, and the images created by artists reflect that diversity.

Images of Jesus in the Scriptures

Such a multitude of artistic depictions should make us aware that, like God, Jesus cannot be held to one image. The writers of the Christian Testament offer many images themselves. We will look at just a few of them.

◆   As you read on, consider the role each image of Jesus might play in prayer. Which image comes most easily to mind when you pray? Do any images inhibit your prayer? What image best represents Jesus for you?

Emmanuel, God-with-Us

In the Gospel according to Matthew, Joseph has a dream in which he is advised to marry the young woman Mary even though she is pregnant, because the child within her is from the Holy Spirit. Matthew adds that all this happened

> to fulfill what had been spoken by the Lord through the prophet [Isaiah]:
>   "Look, the virgin shall conceive and bear a son,
>   and they shall name him Emmanuel,"
> which means, "God is with us." (1:22–23)

The image of Jesus as God-with-us carries through in many other images of Jesus. It reminds us that Jesus embodies God, regardless of the specific image of Jesus we are envisioning. The messenger in Matthew 1:23 refers to Jesus as God-with-us in the months before Jesus' human birth, and Jesus remains God-with-us throughout his childhood, ministry, death, and Resurrection. And he is still with us, right up to the present moment and into the future. Portraying Jesus as God-with-us gives a solid foundation to all other images of Jesus.

The Word of God

The Gospel of John opens with these words: "In the beginning was the Word, and the Word was with God, and the Word was God." Before the appearance of Jesus, the word of God was known through the actions and teachings of God as they are revealed in history—for example, in the liberation of the people of Israel from slavery. In Jesus, however, "the Word became flesh and lived among us, and we have seen his glory, the glory as of a father's only son, full of grace and truth" (John 1:14). That is, the truth of God was given a human form.

Praying with the image of Jesus as word, as the truth of God, can be rewarding in times of discernment—times when we are trying to envision the direction of our life, for example, or when we are struggling to make a conscientious choice about a moral issue. It can help us to be open to God's truth, embodied in the words and actions of Jesus.

Jesus as Light and Way

Jesus was no stranger to metaphors. He used them himself to describe his identity and mission. As a teacher, Jesus knew the writings of the prophets and was most likely aware that the prophet Isaiah had compared God to light. Jesus described himself with that image as well: "'I am the light of the world. Whoever follows me will never walk in darkness but will have the light of life'" (John 8:12).

Isaiah's image of God as light helps us to envision God also as a guide. Jesus, too, describes himself as a guide. Later in John's Gospel, Jesus is asked by his disciple Thomas, "'How can we know the way [to God]?'" (14:5). Jesus responds: "'I am the way, and the truth, and the life. No one comes to the Father except through me. If you know me, you will know my Father also'" (verses 6–7).

As light and way, Jesus' image is that of the ultimate guide—the one who shows us, and is, the way to God. In prayer this image of Jesus helps us to consider the words and actions of Jesus that made him both light and way. Reflecting on these aspects of his life can enrich our own words and actions.

Teacher, Servant, and Friend

Throughout the Gospels Jesus is often addressed as Teacher, Master, Rabbi. He acknowledges his role as teacher, but his own understanding of this role was probably quite different from the understanding of other teachers in his time. Jesus the teacher spoke and preached with authority and confidence, and that was obvious to people. But he did not act in an authoritarian, or domineering, manner. At the Last Supper, Jesus insisted on washing the feet of his disciples—a task generally done by a servant, not a teacher. He explained to his disciples:

> "You call me Teacher and Lord—and you are right, for that is what I am. So if I, your Lord and Teacher, have washed your feet, you also ought to wash one another's feet. For I have set you an example, that you also should do as I have done to you." (John 13:13–15)

Jesus served his students humbly and effectively, and expected them to follow his example.

At the same time, Jesus called his disciples friends and considered himself their friend. He said to his disciples:

> "You are my friends if you do what I command you. I do not call you servants any longer, because the servant does not know what the master is doing; but I have called you friends, because I have made known to you everything that I have heard from my Father." (John 15:14–15)

The image of Jesus as a caring, loving friend is a natural image for prayer, one that may come readily to you. To approach Jesus in prayer as a friend is to approach the one who makes known to us all that he has heard from God.

Jesus as Bread

When Christians celebrate the Eucharist, Jesus is envisioned as bread. This image, like others, comes directly from

Jesus, who said: "'I am the bread of life. Whoever comes to me will never be hungry, and whoever believes in me will never be thirsty'" (John 6:35).

Jesus as the bread of life is a rich and vivid image. Bread is a basic food. It is not surprising, then, that when Jesus instructed his disciples about how to remember his presence, he shared bread with them: "Then he took a loaf of bread, and when he had given thanks, he broke it and gave it to them, saying, 'This is my body, which is given for you. Do this in remembrance of me'" (Luke 22:19).

The celebration of the Eucharist is the high point of the church's prayer. But imaging Jesus as bread is not reserved only for eucharistic celebrations. In a prayer using this image, we may also simply reflect on our own ability to be "bread" for others.

◆ How are you nourishing and caring for others? How are you bread in your world?

Reflecting on Images of Jesus

As with images of God, when we reflect on the many images of Jesus that are offered in the Scriptures, we will probably see some that are familiar and others that are new to us.

◆ What image of Jesus comes to mind when you settle into a moment of quiet reflection? Does a different image appear when you pray in a group or at church? Take notice of the images of Jesus around you, and bring them into your prayer.

Praying with the Holy Spirit

Of the three persons of the Trinity, the Holy Spirit is perhaps the most difficult to imagine. Again, the Holy Spirit is the love that exists between the Father and the Son, the First and Second Persons of the Trinity. The Spirit dwells within the human heart and enables us to perceive the presence of the Creator and Redeemer. The Spirit also enlivens our images of God and Jesus and enables us to pray from the heart.

Images of the Spirit in the Scriptures

The Christian Testament contains images of the Spirit that can help us to understand the presence and action of the Spirit, which is a good starting point for prayer.

The Baptism of Jesus: The Spirit "Like a Dove"

In all the Gospel accounts, the baptism of Jesus by John is the occasion for the Spirit to be present. Luke tells the story in this way:

> Now when all the people were baptized, and when Jesus also had been baptized and was praying, the heaven was opened, and the Holy Spirit descended upon him in bodily form like a dove. And a voice came from heaven, "You are my Son, the Beloved; with you I am well pleased." (Luke 3:21–22)

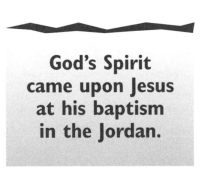

God's Spirit came upon Jesus at his baptism in the Jordan.

The Gospel stories about this event have led to the use of a dove to symbolize the Spirit.

◆ What are some dovelike traits that make this image of the Spirit helpful?

Jesus' Promise: The Spirit as Advocate

During some of his final moments with his disciples, Jesus told them that although he would no longer be among them in the flesh, the Holy Spirit would come to them and remain with them to guide them: "'And I will ask the Father, and he will give you another Advocate, to be with you forever. This is the Spirit of truth'" (John 14:16–17).

The Greek word for "advocate" is *paraclete,* which can also be translated as "helper," "intercessor," "counselor," and "protector." By sending the Advocate, Jesus is promising that the Holy Spirit will guide, defend, and uphold all who follow his commands. When praying with the Holy Spirit, any of these meanings or names that describe the Spirit may be used as images.

◆ Recall some circumstances in which you needed the help of the Spirit as advocate?

◆ Have you ever come through a difficult experience successfully and felt as though you received guidance from an unknown source? How could you prayerfully thank the Advocate?

Pentecost: The Spirit as Wind and Fire

The Pentecost experience demonstrates the dramatic, empowering effect of the Spirit. In the Pentecost story in the Acts of the Apostles, different people encounter the Spirit in different ways, and the Spirit clearly enlivens all who are present:

> When the day of Pentecost had come, they were all together in one place. And suddenly from heaven there came a sound like the rush of a violent wind, and it filled the entire house where they were sitting. Divided tongues, as of fire, appeared among them, and a tongue rested on each of them. All of them were filled with the Holy Spirit and began to speak in other languages, as the Spirit gave them ability. (2:1–4)

This vivid passage shows us the Spirit dynamically active. The passage also gives us images with which we can pray: the Spirit as wind and fire, moving, breathing, transforming, giving warmth and light. These images have been used for centuries to symbolize the Spirit in art and as ways to address or call on the Spirit in prayer.

◆ Imagine a way in which the Spirit as wind and fire could empower you as the people were empowered at the first Pentecost. If you need emotional strength right now, pray to the Spirit as wind or fire.

Images of the Spirit Within Our Heart

To pray with the Holy Spirit is to pray with the person of the Trinity who is very close to us, sent by Jesus to dwell in our heart. The Spirit dwells in us as individuals and in the community of believers. When we image God the Father or Mother, or Jesus as part of our prayer, the Spirit, in our heart, animates that image, making it vivid and real. In a way, no matter how we pray—alone or in a group, giving praise or seeking help, focusing on Jesus or focusing on God the Creator—the Spirit is always present in our prayer.

Saint Paul reminds us, "Your body is a temple [sanctuary] of the Holy Spirit within you" (1 Corinthians 6:19). Paul paints a wonderful picture of the Spirit praying for us within us:

> Likewise the Spirit helps us in our weakness; for we do not know how to pray as we ought, but that very Spirit intercedes with sighs too deep for words. And God, who searches the heart, knows what is the mind of the Spirit, because the Spirit intercedes for the saints [the faithful] according to the will of God. (Romans 8:26–27)

The Ocean of God

God is a mystery who can never be understood completely, so it is natural that we should use metaphors and images to talk about God. When we pray, these images can focus our prayer on an aspect of God that has real meaning for us.

If we pray to God as an infinite, unknowable mystery, we are likely to feel that our prayer is ineffective and does not really address God. We need a more tangible image of God. When it comes to understanding God and encountering God in prayer, we are much like children at the beach. The children cannot possibly understand or play with the entire ocean, but they *can* see and hear the wave that crashes in front of them, they *can* feel the cold water that rushes up and touches their feet. They will never know the whole sea, but they *can* go home and say, "I touched the ocean."

4

PETITION

ASKING GOD FOR HELP

People who live prayerfully, responding to God in all of their life, are not constantly "saying prayers." But the occasions when they do consciously pray nourish the rest of their life. Because they turn their attention deliberately to God at certain focused times, they carry in themselves a prayerful spirit, a heart that is open to God and sensitive to the sacred even when they are not intentionally and knowingly praying.

"Please, God . . ."

Perhaps the most familiar way that we consciously pray is to ask God for help. This is called prayer of petition. From our earliest years, most of us use this simple, trusting way of approaching God. Do these prayers sound familiar?

- Please, God, help me get through this day.
- God, help us in this difficulty.
- Dear God, keep my children safe.
- God, let me get this job; I'd give anything for it!
- Please, God, help me know what to say when I have to face my boss.

Prayer of petition is familiar to most of us. It is the form of prayer that comes most easily and naturally to many people and may be the form that comes to mind when most people hear the word *prayer*. However, asking God for things is only one among many kinds of Christian prayer. If we never get beyond it to other ways of relating to God, our prayer life is somewhat limited, just as a friendship is rather stunted if the only way two friends can relate is for one to ask favors of the other. Nevertheless, asking God for help is a genuine form of prayer.

Why should we tell God our needs? For one reason, God desires a deep relationship with us and is longing to hear from us. God wants us to pour out our daily needs, sharing all the little details of our life as we would with our best friend. When we bring the stuff of our everyday life to God, asking for help, we are really saying to God: "I love you. I trust you. I need you." We recognize our own dependence on God and remember that every gift, even life itself, comes from God.

Pouring out our needs to God, then, is not simply for children; it is for all of us. God loves to hear from us, delights in our asking, and responds with warmth and tenderness to our prayer. Jesus himself taught his followers this when he said:

> "Ask, and it will be given you; search, and you will find; knock, and the door will be opened for you. For everyone who asks receives, and everyone who searches finds, and for everyone who knocks, the door will be opened. . . . If you . . . know how to give good gifts to your children, how much more will your Father in heaven give good things to those who ask him!" (Matthew 7:7–11)

In the Christian understanding of prayers of petition, we ask God's help through Jesus. That is why prayers in the official liturgy usually end with the phrase "in Jesus' name" or "through Jesus Christ."

◆ When you were young, what kinds of needs did you pray for?
◆ What personal needs do you, or could you, pray to God about now? How have your needs changed over the years?

How Does God Answer Prayers?

Several people talk about what kinds of "answers" they expect when they pray to God for help:

- I expect God to take care of the problem in a way God sees fit. There is no sure way of telling, only a sixth sense sort of thing.
- I expect an answer even if God just gives me the strength to deal with the problem myself. I know the prayer is answered if the problem is resolved or made easier to deal with.
- I expect to be relieved of some burden. However, I do not expect this burden to magically disappear; only through hard work will it be gone.
- I expect God to listen to me. Just praying for something makes me feel better. It's as if there is nothing to worry about.

Indeed, prayer is answered in many ways. Sometimes the response comes as a resolution we had not anticipated. It may take the form of changing our own heart so that we understand the situation better and can cope with it. Even the act of praying in itself can become an answer, because articulating our needs helps us understand ourselves better. And, too, at times the thing we pray for fervently is given to us: a successful outcome of a project, a cure of a child's or parent's illness, and so on.

But our experience suggests that we may not get all our prayers answered. Sometimes it seems that God is ignoring us. In spite of our intense pleas to God, our company loses a major contract, or someone we care for very much does not feel the same way about us, or our friends get divorced. Does this mean that God has not answered our prayers?

That very difficult question has no ready responses. We know from Jesus' words that God hears our prayers, but we also know that not every prayer in the human heart is consistent with God's will. The Lord's Prayer—the basic, fundamental prayer taught by Jesus—has as its first petition that God's reign of justice, peace, and love may become a reality in our world. In the Lord's Prayer, we pray, "Thy kingdom come. / Thy will be done on earth, as it is in heaven."

When we share our personal needs with God, then, it is understood that the overriding need is for God's Reign to come and God's will to be done among all creation, now and in the future. How that is happening and will happen is not always obvious to us. God's action in the world is not restricted to our own notions of what it should be.

◆ Do you believe that God answers prayers? If so, in what ways have you experienced God's answers?

God's Will and Human Freedom

Part of the mystery of how God's Reign ultimately will come about is that it cannot be accomplished apart from human freedom. God works *with* human beings and their freedom. No matter how much we pray for the stopping of some evil, such as a war or the slaughter of innocent people, God will not force the hands of the persons responsible for that evil. If God canceled out their freedom, God would not be God, and the persons would not be human. God can move people's hearts in powerful ways, but God's will does not happen magically. It happens through human beings who freely choose and take action.

Persons who have the attitude that prayer is magical can become very passive, a bit like the man in this story:

> A devout religious man fell on hard times. So he took to praying in the following fashion: "Lord, remember all the years I served you as best I could, asking for nothing in return. Now that I am old and bankrupt I am going to ask you for a favor for the first time in my life and I am sure you will not say no. Allow me to win the lottery."
>
> Days passed. Then weeks and months. But nothing happened. Finally, almost driven to despair, he cried out one night, "Why don't you give me a break, God?"
>
> He suddenly heard the voice of God replying, "Give me a break yourself! Why don't you buy a lottery ticket?" (Anthony de Mello, *Taking Flight,* pages 103–104)

In other words, God's will cannot be accomplished without our taking action!

◆ Translate the story of the devout religious man into an example of a person who prays for something but fails to "buy a lottery ticket."

Closer to God's Heart

As limited human beings, we are not completely, or even nearly, in touch with God's heart. Our methods are often not God's, nor is our timing. We are capable of astonishing self-deception about what is good for us. We cannot possibly know all that God knows, see as God sees, love as God loves. But we can grow closer to Jesus—who is God-made-flesh, God-with-us as a human being.

Through praying, reflecting on Jesus' life and message, meeting Jesus in the sacraments, and uniting our everyday life with Jesus', over time we can begin to pray and hope and dream as Jesus did. If we are open, God's grace, poured out to us in Jesus, will fill us and transform us little by little. Our prayers of petition may begin to include asking God for forgiveness, asking God to soften our heart or to open our eyes.

In this transforming way, gradually we will "become" Jesus, at least to the extent that our limits allow, and grow closer to the heart of God. If we were to become totally one with Jesus, our own heart would be so united with God's that we would always pray for what God wants. Jesus said as much to his disciples: "'If you abide in me, and my words abide in you, ask for whatever you wish, and it will be done for you'" (John 15:7).

> **If we are open, God's grace will fill us and transform us little by little.**

Discernment: Seeking God's Will in Decisions

Many Christians over the centuries have tried to unite themselves with God's heart, particularly when they are making significant choices. In decision making, the process of seeking the direction or alternative that God would want is called discernment.

John Baptist de La Salle, who founded the Brothers of the Christian Schools in the seventeenth century, outlined steps that can help us today when we try to seek God's will:

1. . . . Acknowledge that Jesus is with you now and explain to him all the facets of the decision [you need to make] or situation [that is causing you confusion]: the who, what, when, where, how, and why.
2. Listen to Jesus' response. One way of doing this is to recall biblical stories related to your situation. Another is to search the Gospels and the Epistles for the advice Jesus has for you. Each page is filled with infinite wisdom.
3. After you have listened to Jesus, talk with him some more in prayer.
4. If you need more clarity, discuss the decision or situation with someone you trust and who can help you.
5. Spend more time asking for the guidance of the Holy Spirit.
6. Decide, act, and monitor the results, knowing that God will help you.
7. If things go well, rejoice in your God. If the decision proves wrong or the situation cannot be resolved, trust that God is still with you and wishes you to grow in some way. Discern once again. God is merciful.

(Carl Koch, *Praying with John Baptist de La Salle,* page 51)

◆ Use De La Salle's steps for a meditation on some decision you need to make or a situation that is causing you confusion. Focus on just one decision or situation.

When Prayer Seems Unanswered

Let's return to the dilemma we face when we ask God for something and God does not seem to answer us. The following people have struggled with this situation. Their comments show that they realize that sometimes their prayer was too limited, and that God did answer it, but on a deeper level than they asked for:

- I remember being glad for not getting the answer to my prayers. I had prayed that I would not get transferred. I'm glad now that we did have to move because we have had opportunities for growth that were not present in the first situation.
- I was glad when I did not get back together with my ex-fiancé because that helped me to grow stronger mentally and become less dependent on one person. Also, the relationship would have suffered eventually, because he was always looking for attention from other women.
- When my wife was pregnant with our first child, my grandfather was really sick. I prayed that he wouldn't die. He died, but then I realized it was for the best. Living was only prolonging his suffering. When he died, he was at peace.

All these persons discovered something of the paradox of the paschal mystery—that new life can come through loss and suffering, not simply from our own notions of what is best. Embracing the paschal mystery is the way we expand our heart and grow into God's heart.

◆   Think of a time that you prayed for something but did not get what you wanted. How can reflection on the paschal mystery help you take a deeper look at the situation?

It's Okay to Ask *Why*

When things do not work out our way, we may try hard to make sense of them. We may come to see the wisdom of a situation over time. In some instances, though, we cannot make any sense of it at all, and we are driven to cry out, *"Why,* God?": *"Why* did I not get the job even though I was suitably qualified?"; *"Why* did my sister die so young?" God does not mind our asking *why.* Sometimes it is the only way we have to express the pain we feel, and God can handle it.

It is also human to live with questions that are unresolved. When we are faced with some incomprehensible anguish, we can beg to know why, but we should not assume that God has "arranged" or "intended" that suffering for us and that we simply have to figure out God's "reasoning"; God never wills our pain. Instead we can acknowledge the mystery of suffering and place ourselves in the hands of God, who is with us in our deepest distress. We can put our hope in God, knowing that God *ultimately* will bring forth goodness and life even from the most painful circumstances.

◆ If you have ever felt like crying, "Why, God?" over some suffering or injustice you could not make sense of, did you tell God how you felt?

Loving Others Through Intercessory Prayer

A woman named Amy describes an experience with a young friend who has been in terrible emotional distress:

> I've spent hours with Katie, going over and over all the awful things that have happened to her in the last couple months. First, there's her parents' splitting up. That started her going downhill. After that, her boyfriend told her he couldn't deal with her bad moods anymore, and he dumped her. Then she started sliding in her tests and her homework, and she just got told she's flunking biology and algebra. We have talked and talked, and I've tried to coach her through it all. I'd give anything to make it better for her. But I haven't been able to.
>
> Last night, I was lying in bed thinking and worrying about Katie, and I couldn't get to sleep. But then I decided I would try praying about Katie. My prayer was: "Dear God, please be with Katie and let her know she's not alone. Help her handle all these problems and help me know what I can do for her. I love Katie, but I don't know what else to do right now except to turn to you. So, God, I'm putting Katie in your hands."

Amy's simple words to God are a prayer of intercession.

A Way to Love Through God

When we offer a prayer of intercession for someone, we are simply asking God's help for that person. Making a prayer of intercession is a way of expressing our love for that person, in order to unite ourselves with God and let God's love flow through us to the person we are praying for. We may ask for something specific for that person, like help with parenting or the motivation to quit an addiction. Or we may simply reach out to that person in prayer,

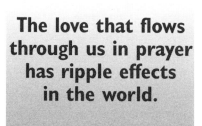

The love that flows through us in prayer has ripple effects in the world.

uniting ourselves with God to bring God's love to him or her. Prayer of intercession gives us a way to magnify our love by uniting it with God's own love.

We should not underestimate the power of intercessory prayer. It is not that God has a change of mind and decides to love the person after all, whereas before God was indifferent. Our prayer does not alter God's love, which is always present and active. But it does change our own relationship with God and with the person we are praying for. Through prayer we establish a bond with that person that was not there before, even if we tried hard to help him or her. We allow ourselves to be a channel of God's love for that person, and that will forever change us and the person.

We may not see an immediate effect in the person or situation we are praying for, but that does not mean our prayer was powerless. We have no idea of the ripple effects of the love we allow to flow through us in prayer. In a sense the whole world is different because of our prayer.

After the night of her prayer, Amy may find she is more serene in talking with Katie, and that may help Katie feel less desperate. Amy may then take Katie into her concern every night in prayer. She may even do a kind of meditative intercessory prayer, in which she imagines that she and Jesus are with Katie in her room, giving Katie comfort and peace. After that, Amy may realize God's presence when she is actually with Katie and may feel guided in what she is saying to Katie. We cannot assume a "happy ending" to the situation, but we do know that Amy's prayer will make a difference. Love is never wasted.

Pray for Whom?

The potential for intercessory prayer is as wide as the universe. First we are drawn to pray for those who are closest and most beloved to us—our family and friends. As we are united more and more with Jesus, we will find that our circle of concern goes further and further out, embracing acquaintances and even strangers who seem to need prayer. A supervisor who has been working very hard, or a grocery store clerk who looks hassled, or a little kid on the street who seems upset might become a subject for our prayer.

Prayer of intercession can extend to anyone anytime. Of particular concern to Christians are poor and suffering people, people who are sick and dying, all those who are particularly vulnerable or weak. We can pray for the victims of war or of discrimination. We can pray for homeless people, people with AIDS, hungry people, prisoners, women who are unmarried and pregnant, drug-addicted people, all those who feel lonely and forgotten. Leaders in politics, church, school, or work need our prayers, even—perhaps especially—when we are unhappy with their leadership. Leaders carry pressures and responsibilities of which we may not be fully aware.

◆ Think of some people who need your prayers. Identify people you know, as well as people you do not know but care about.

Praying for Our Enemies

When Jesus walked among his disciples, one of the most difficult lessons he taught was this: "'You have heard that it was said, "You shall love your neighbor and hate your enemy." But I say to you, Love your enemies and pray for those who persecute you'" (Matthew 5:43–44).

It seems reasonable to pray for those we are close to and for people who are suffering in some way. But what about Jesus' command to pray for our enemies and in fact to love them? We might imagine ourselves choking on a prayer for someone who has been cruel to us. Wouldn't it be an insincere prayer?

When we are entangled in a conflict with someone, or terribly hurt by him or her, we need to recognize that the other person is loved by God just as we are. Rather than gritting our teeth and praying, "God, bless so-and-so, whom I can't stand," we can pray to understand the person with God's own heart: "What makes this person act as he does?"; "What experiences might have caused this?"; "What is the person afraid of?"; "How is this person who hurt me also hurt inside?" We can pray that God's light and peace and love will surround that person and sink in. We can also pray for healing in our relationship with that person, a healing that perhaps can be started only by one person praying for the other.

The world of people and situations we can pray for is wide open because no person or concern is outside the love and care of God.

◆ Focus on a person with whom you have had a conflict. Try praying for that person with God in your heart.

The Communion of Saints

Christians have a way of making intercessory prayer that invites in a whole community of persons who have gone before us in death and are now united with the heart of God. These persons are the saints who have died, and we believe they are very much with us and concerned about us because they share in God's life and concerns. The saints include not only persons officially canonized by the church, but also all persons who are united with God. In fact, in a certain sense, all of us who are trying to do God's will are con-

Those we love who have died are still with us in spirit.

sidered saints. The bond that unites the living and dead saints is called the communion of saints.

You likely love someone who has died. Perhaps you feel at times that this person is with you in spirit, still caring about you and supporting you in your struggles. That experience is a sense of the communion of saints. Christians believe that not only those we personally knew, but all those who have died in God's grace are somehow present to us, advocating for us in the events of life. It is comforting and uplifting to be able to go to God about our special needs in company with these saints, as a community.

A woman's memory of an event in her parish's life illustrates the reality of the communion of saints:

> Joe was dying. And Joe was only 26. I had a few years on him, but death was still a stranger to me, a macabre figure who sometimes lurked at the edge of an accident scene but more often appeared at the bedside of the very old.
>
> Someone had called our pastor. We were welcome to use the church, he said, but none of the parish priests would be home. And so it happened that a group of people gathered in the church on a Sunday afternoon in 1968. Joe's best friend, an ex-seminarian, was familiar with the Church's prayers for the dying; he put that structure to the service of our aching hearts. And we prayed the Litany of the Saints for Joe. "Pray for him," we begged Mary, the patriarchs, the prophets and a long lineup of saints.
>
> And then something strange began to happen. As we worked our way down the list of great saints, I had a sense that the empty pews were filling. Joseph and Andrew and Stephen, Perpetua, Agatha and Catherine, Athanasius and Teresa—one by one they took their places as we called their names. No longer were we a little group of sad and frightened friends. We were part of an immense throng celebrating a grand send-off, speeding Joe home.
>
> For years, I didn't tell anyone how I had watched that church fill. Someone might think I was crazy. I wasn't sure

of my sanity myself. Then one day a priest friend spoke of his ordination. He recalled lying face down on the sanctuary floor, feeling unworthy, uncertain that he would be a good priest, while the assembly prayed the Litany of the Saints. Suddenly he felt greatly consoled in being part of this great communion of saints—the living assembly surrounding him as well as the great saints of the past who were being invoked. These saintly brothers and sisters comforted, sustained and reassured him that he was not alone.

So I'm not mad after all. *Communion* and *community* are two words with one root—two words for one reality: people who love and support one another. (Carol Luebering, "A Supportive Community," *Catholic Update,* November 1987)

◆ Do you love someone who has died and who still seems present to you? Reflect on the ways that person still seems to be with you.

◆ Think of some people who died in the distant or recent past and who are like advocates for all humanity. Consider in what way each one might be working on our behalf.

Trusting God Always

The point of making prayers of petition and intercessory prayers is not to try to control life more effectively by "getting God on our side." God is on our side, always and everywhere. Likewise, the reason we try to discern God's will is not so that we can have certainty and assurance that our actions will "pay off." Asking God for help is about trusting God and growing in the ways of God, not controlling God or trying to bargain with God.

All our efforts to seek God's will and ask for God's help are really just ways of learning to trust God more deeply, in whatever uncertain or perilous circumstances we may find ourselves. In that spirit of trust, let's offer to God all our concerns about what lies ahead, with this prayer:

Dear God, sometimes I wonder
 Where am I going?
 What's my life leading to?
 Is everything going to turn out well?
When the road ahead looks uncertain or fearful
 and I don't know where I'm going,
Let me yearn to be on the path you want for me.
Then I believe you will bless my yearning
 and be with me every step of the way,
 even in trouble, danger, and sorrow.
I trust that you will lead me along the way
 that brings me, finally, to the greatest joy.

5

THANKS AND PRAISE

GIVING GOD A JOYFUL HEART

When we ask for God's help, as in a prayer of petition, we are really expressing our trust in God. We are putting our life in God's hands.

God, of course, has always been there surrounding us with love, even long before we ever thought to ask for help.

All Is a Gift

Everything in life—every moment and circumstance of our existence—is a gift from God. Gratitude is the most natural response to the giftedness of life. But it takes a sense of openness and wonder to recognize that. In an ordinary frame of mind, we tend to take life and the world for granted.

Opening Our Eyes

A crisis or a brush with death can open our eyes to the gift of life as can nothing else. Here is an account of one woman's enlightening experience:

> When my boys were fifteen and thirteen, there was a lot of tension between the boys and myself. This carried over to the relationship I had with my husband, as we often disagreed on how we should handle the boys. During this same period, I was struggling to care for my aging parents, and my husband was personnel manager for a company that was downsizing. So, needless to say, it was not a great time for us.
>
> At Christmas we took a trip halfway across the country to see my in-laws in South Dakota. The weather conditions were going to be bad for driving, but that year we decided to go anyway.
>
> Everything went safely until the trip home. The temperature was about zero, and my husband, who was driving, hit an ice patch on the road. The next thing I knew, the car was spinning around and then rolling over and over. We finally landed upside down. I was sure that we would all die. But we didn't; all we had were some bumps and bruises. I had a big black eye. It was so incredible. There we all were, looking at one another in the snow, embracing each other warmly, amazed that we had made it without any personal disaster.
>
> Something really different happened to our family from the minute we climbed out of the wreck. We all felt so grateful for one another and for everything in life. We were just standing there, and I remember thinking, This snow looks beautiful, and the blue sky, and I don't even mind that it's freezing cold, the air just feels so good on my face. Some kind people stopped to help us. We went to a motel, and we were all attentive to one another and

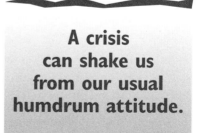

A crisis can shake us from our usual humdrum attitude.

were just glad to be with one another. My husband and I weren't our usual irritated selves, and the boys had matured in an hour. We had the best time in the motel together. It felt like we suddenly had this whole new world and life ahead of us, and we didn't want to take it for granted. Like God had given us this huge gift, and we just had to appreciate it and live according to it.

That sense of wonder at the goodness of life, even life with troubles, characterizes the person with a grateful heart. A crisis can shake us from our usual humdrum outlook to see the world in a fresh, new way, with gratitude. Maybe that is because a crisis or a brush with death gets our attention, forces us to stop and be present to what life is all about for a while.

◆   Have you ever been in a crisis that shook you out of your usual way of looking at the world? What happened?

Missing the Obvious

When we are restlessly moving from experience to experience, searching for something more out of life, we often cannot appreciate what is right before us. We are a bit like the younger ocean fish in this little story:

"Excuse me," said an ocean fish.
"You are older than I, so
can you tell me where to find
this thing they call the ocean?"

"The ocean," said the older fish, "is the thing
you are in now."

"Oh, this? But this is water. What I'm seeking
is the ocean," said the disappointed fish
as he swam away to search elsewhere.

(Anthony de Mello, *The Song of the Bird,* page 12)

While searching for good things that we hope will make our life happier or give our life meaning, we may miss the obvious—God's overwhelming graciousness to us. Most of the time we are not aware of being surrounded with a gift so great and mysterious. In fact, we are "swimming" in the gift! But our spontaneous attitude is usually wishful and restless, rather than grateful.

 Think of how you might be missing the obvious—seeing the water but not the ocean around you.

Why Not Gratitude?

Why do we seem to find it so difficult or unusual to experience life as a gift that calls forth a spirit of thankfulness in us? What is it that keeps us from seeing the totality of what we have been given, like the fish that cannot perceive the ocean, but can see only the water?

Contemporary society, unfortunately, fosters a blindness to the understanding that reality is totally *given* to us. Some of society's values and attitudes work directly against a spirit of gratitude.

A Worship of Independence

A fundamental value in our society is the ability to say: "Whatever I have, I have earned. I am self-made. I don't owe anyone anything, and I don't want to." Given such a worship of independence, it goes against the cultural grain to see everything we have and all that we are as essentially a gift.

It is not that giving and receiving are absent in our contemporary world. But they are carefully monitored to prevent our feeling that we "owe" anyone anything. A sense of a "balance sheet" governs relationships: If you help me, I will help you. If you send me a gift for my birthday, I'll send you one for yours. We tend to feel uncomfortable when things are out of balance. We say, "Thank you," for gifts or favors out of politeness, but often with a view to evening up the score. We do not like to feel obligated to anyone, as that threatens our sense of control.

◆ Where have you seen or felt the worship of independence?
◆ Do you have difficulty seeing everything you have and all that you are as a gift? Why or why not?

Ourselves at the Center

Contemporary values put us human beings at the center of the universe: The world is made for us and, by implication, for me personally. I am *owed* everything I have. I have a right to the best, a right to be treated well. When something good happens to me, it is because I deserve it, not because of anyone's graciousness to me. This attitude is really just another way of feeling independent and in control.

The sense that all of life and everything I have is a marvelous gift given to me, one I did not earn and do not necessarily deserve, is indeed a strange and fresh notion in our society. It is also the core of a grateful and humble heart.

Humility: Recognizing Who We Are

Humility is an approach to life and the world that is fundamentally different from the dominant societal values. The virtue of humility, contrary to our possible misunderstandings of it, has nothing to do with putting ourselves down or refusing to recognize our talents. Humble persons do not respond to a compliment on a well-done job or performance by shrugging it off, as in, "Oh, no, it really wasn't anything" or "I hardly knew what I was doing."

Instead, humble persons recognize and accept who they are, with all their strengths, talents, and weaknesses. They are realistic about themselves, neither inflating their abilities and achievements nor downplaying them. But the humble person is deeply convinced that everything he or she has is a gift from God to be shared, not a hard-won possession to be hoarded. The humble person knows that the center of the universe is not himself or herself, but God. Without humility, we find ourselves choking on gratitude, mouthing the words of thanks but not feeling sincerely thankful to God.

◆ Does the description of humility given here differ from the one you have held in your mind?

◆ How might you cultivate humility in your own life?

A Grateful, Praise-Filled People

The Christian heritage has been one of gratitude and praise, beginning with our spiritual ancestors, the Jews, and continuing in the early Christian communities.

The Ancient Jews

Our ancestors in the Jewish faith experienced all of creation and all of life as a gift. Despite times of persecution and suffering, faithful Jews could still sing songs of praise and gratitude. Many of these songs are the psalms that we know from the Hebrew Scriptures. The following excerpts express the Israelites' grateful delight in creation:

> Bless the LORD, O my soul.
> > O LORD my God, you are very great.
>
> > > > (Verse 1)
>
> You make springs gush forth in the valleys;
> > they flow between the hills,
> giving drink to every wild animal;
> . . . .
> You cause the grass to grow for the cattle,
> > and plants for people to use,
> to bring forth food from the earth,
> > and wine to gladden the human heart,
> oil to make the face shine,
> > and bread to strengthen the human heart.
>
> > > > (Psalm 104:10–15)

The Israelites also thanked God over and over for the way God had worked for them as a people. In Psalm 136 they sang out their praise and thanks for being rescued from slavery in Egypt and brought into freedom in the Promised Land:

> O give thanks to the LORD, for he is good,
> > for his steadfast love endures forever.
>
> > > > (Verse 1)
>
> who divided the Red Sea in two,
> > for his steadfast love endures forever;

and made Israel pass through the midst of it,
    for his steadfast love endures forever;
but overthrew Pharaoh and his army in the Red Sea,
    for his steadfast love endures forever;
who led his people through the wilderness,
    for his steadfast love endures forever;

.   .   .   .

and gave their land as a heritage,
    for his steadfast love endures forever;
a heritage to his servant Israel,
    for his steadfast love endures forever.

(Verses 13–22)

The faithful ancient Jews took nothing for granted. From the grass growing in the field to their migration into a promising, fertile land, they saw all things as coming from the hand of God.

◆ Go outside, no matter what the weather, and look around you at creation. Notice both great and small wonders, and give thanks to God for each of them.
◆ Recall an experience when you felt that God was at work in your life. Pour out your thanks for what God did for you.

The Early Christians

Centuries after the psalms were first sung by the Israelites, the early Christian communities were filled with the same grateful spirit and prayed the same sacred hymns. Saint Paul told the Christians of the city of Ephesus:

Sing psalms and hymns and spiritual songs among yourselves, singing and making melody to the Lord in your hearts, giving thanks to God the Father at all times and for everything in the name of our Lord Jesus Christ. (Ephesians 5:19–20)

Like their spiritual ancestors, the Jews, who recalled gratefully that God had freed them from the death of slavery and brought them to life in the Promised Land, the early Christians poured out their thanks to God for bringing them from death to life through Jesus. The Eucharist, the meal that the early Christians shared in remembrance of Jesus, was actually a pouring out of thanks and praise for all that God had done for them. (The Greek word *eucharist* means "thanksgiving.") This passage from the Acts of the Apostles portrays a sharing, praising community in Jerusalem that expressed its joy in the "breaking of bread," or the Eucharist:

> They devoted themselves to the apostles' teaching and fellowship, to the breaking of bread and the prayers.
>
> Awe came upon everyone, because many wonders and signs were being done by the apostles. All who believed were together and had all things in common; they would sell their possessions and goods and distribute the proceeds to all, as any had need. Day by day, as they spent much time together in the temple, they broke bread at home and ate their food with glad and generous hearts, praising God and having the goodwill of all the people. And day by day the Lord added to their number those who were being saved. (2:42–47)

Growing in Gratitude

We come from a religious tradition that is saturated with thanks and praise. This tradition also suggests how we can grow into a more grateful spirit.

Wake Up to Surprise

If you are having trouble getting in touch with the sense of gratefulness that will fill you with wonder and humility, try this: *Allow yourself to be surprised*. Let yourself stop long enough to notice a rainbow or the first snow of winter or the first buds of spring or a sunset. Be present where you are. Whatever makes you catch your breath—the smile of a baby, a beautiful song, the touch of a friend—savor it with wonder, with amazed admiration.

> **Whatever makes you catch your breath—savor it with wonder.**

Surprise is the beginning of gratefulness, a kind of rousing that we may need to get accustomed to as a gradual way into gratitude. One spiritual writer says it wisely:

> Once we wake up in this way, we can strive to stay awake. Then we can allow ourselves to become more and more awakened. Waking up is a process. In the morning it is quite a different process for different people. Some of us wake up with a start and are wide awake for the rest of the day. They are lucky. Others have to do it stage by stage, cup of coffee by cup of coffee. What counts is that we don't go back to bed again. What counts on your path to fulfillment is that we remember the great truth that moments of surprise want to teach us: everything is gratuitous, everything is gift. The degree to which we are awake to this truth is the measure of our gratefulness. And gratefulness is the measure of our aliveness. (Steindl-Rast, *Gratefulness,* pages 11–12)

Treasure the Gift

Once we are "awake" to life as a gift, we will want to stay awake. We can do this by treasuring the gift of life with all our heart, as Sheila treasured a special gift from her grandmother:

> Sheila reached for the little box under the tree. It was wrapped with Grandma Tighe's usual tissue paper, her trademark in Christmas gifts. Sheila flashed a smile at her grandmother across the room and called out: "From you to me, Grandma! Good things come in small packages!" The older woman sat there with peaceful anticipation on her face.
>
> As Sheila carefully unwrapped the tissue paper, she wondered if the present could be earrings, or maybe a gold chain. She never expected it to be the thin gold band that her grandmother had first showed her fifteen years ago, when she was seven. But there it was, in front of her now. Sheila was flooded with feelings for her grandmother, and she jumped up to give her a teary hug. Grandma's eyes were brimming too.
>
> The band was Grandma Tighe's first wedding ring, given to her by Grandpa Tighe when they married. Sheila

had heard over and over the story of how Grandma and Grandpa had been too poor to afford the diamond set Grandma now wore. She knew that Grandma Tighe cherished the small gold band more than the fancy set her husband gave her after years of working his way up in his company. The little gold ring brought back memories of their first, glorious days of love.

Grandma Tighe had always felt a special kinship and affection for Sheila. Sheila's daring mind and forthrightness reminded her of herself as a girl. Sheila was frequently misunderstood by teachers, other adults, and even peers who didn't quite know what to make of someone so confident, sharp, and challenging. So when Grandma Tighe contemplated a gift for Sheila, the old ring came to mind. It was precious to her, and Sheila knew that. She hoped that Sheila would treasure it too. Seeing her granddaughter slip the ring on, gaze at it with tender admiration, and hold it to her heart, Grandma Tighe knew she had made the right decision.

Sheila loved her grandmother. They understood each other. Sheila thanked and praised Grandma Tighe by treasuring the gift she had been given because she knew how much it meant to her grandmother.

In a similar way, we grow in gratitude to God when we treasure the life and the whole world that we are given. We know that God created everything out of love, and in giving us creation, God is sharing what is precious to God. Like Grandma Tighe's gift of the old wedding band to Sheila, God's gift of life to us must be held to our heart and cherished.

◆ In what ways can you treasure the gift of your own life?
◆ How can you treasure creation?

Find the Gift Even in Suffering

Once we are used to letting gratitude well up in us for the gifts that give us happiness, we have another challenge—the real test of a grateful heart. That is the challenge to "give thanks in all circumstances," in the words of Saint Paul (1 Thessalonians 5:18). How can we be grateful even for things that are going badly for us? This sounds unnatural and even deceitful, like wearing a smile for every occasion.

But this kind of gratitude is not phony; it is profound. It takes deep faith in the paschal mystery—the mystery that life and growth come through death and suffering—to be able to "give thanks in all circumstances." The bedrock trust that God is bringing forth life even out of death does not come to us quickly or readily. For most of us, it is a faith we are led into only gradually by the grace of God. But we can grow into this faith in the movement of death to life. Consider these examples:

- A woman addicted to drugs finds her life transformed when she goes through treatment.
- Friends who stop talking to each other out of anger discover later how important their relationship is when they seek one another out and reconcile.
- A man who is compulsive and driven has a heart attack, which makes him stop for the first time to appreciate his family, his friends, the beauty of flowers, music.

The simple belief that God is loving us in the midst of our suffering can sustain us even when we see no relief from the pain or no purpose to it. Archbishop Desmond Tutu helped lead South Africans to abolish apartheid in their country. He tells of his experience:

> You . . . meet so many wonderful people, people who have suffered and remained faithful. One such person is a man I met when I was praying with the people in Mogopa one night. [Mogopa was a black village that the white government was "moving" as part of a program to force black populations out of certain areas during the 1980s.] Now this is someone whose house was going to be demolished the next day. Clinics, churches, and shops had been demolished already. And the people were going to be moved at the point of a gun. And he got up, and he prayed, in the middle of the night, "God, thank you for loving us."
>
> You couldn't have heard a more nonsensical prayer in the middle of that kind of situation. And yet, here was a man who didn't seem to know any theology but who could offer a prayer of thanksgiving. ("Deeper into God," in Jim Wallis and Joyce Hollyday, editors, *Cloud of Witnesses,* page 77)

Who knows what were the ripple effects of this Mogopa man's simple faith and gratitude in the midst of suffering. Perhaps, in some mysterious way, his grateful spirit helped to bring down apartheid.

 Think of a situation in which you or those you love are experiencing hardship and suffering. Try to offer a sincere prayer of gratitude.

Live in Joy

The fruit of a grateful heart is joy; the root of joy is gratefulness. This joy is not the ordinary kind of happiness that comes because things are going well for us; it runs deeper than that. Like a reliable car engine that purrs steadily no matter what the weather, joy stays with us in all circumstances. Joy is an underground stream that does not dry up even in drought. It is there to water the roots of the trees and bushes in the dry times. Joy stays with us because a grateful heart experiences all of life, not just the good times, as a gift from God.

Do not misunderstand what is meant by joy. A person who is joyful does not necessarily smile constantly or act cheery, bubbly, or jovial. Joy is not a veneer that we can put on to cover our real feelings of sadness or anger. Rather, it is a light shining from within us, radiating a peace and gratitude that is with us even when we are having difficult feelings.

Here is a graphic image of joy that conveys its connection with gratefulness and suffering:

Many years ago I saw a photograph I would never forget: two African children smiling their radiant smiles. And the caption read, "Joy is the gratefulness of God's children." Later, when I traveled in Africa, I rediscovered that smile and the caption came back to me. Everywhere in the world joy is the true expression of gratefulness. But not everywhere are the faces of God's children as transparent to that joy as in black Africa. Nowhere have I seen more radiant joy in children's eyes than in the former Biafra [a part of Nigeria that was in a devastating civil war in the late 1960s]. In [the city of] Enugu I came across groups of children who gather on a busy street corner after dark, set up a small altar, and pray the rosary undisturbed by the hustle and bustle of adults around them. Children, I was told, started that custom during the bloodiest weeks of the war. One generation of children has handed it on to the next for more than a decade. Then it dawned on me that the joy I observed plays on a deep knowledge of suffering as sun-rays play on the surface of dark waterholes. Only a heart familiar with death will appreciate the gift of life with so deep a feeling of joy. (Steindl-Rast, *Gratefulness,* page 18)

◆   Do you know someone who lives in joy? How would you de-scribe that person? What do you think accounts for her or his joy?

An Overflow of Thanksgiving

During the German occupation of the Netherlands, in World War II, a Jewish teenager, Anne Frank, hid with her family in an attic to escape Nazi persecution. Anne later died in a Nazi con-centration camp after her family was discovered. But during the many months the family stayed cooped up in its small shelter, young Anne kept a diary. It has come down to us as her legacy of hope. In the face of so much fear, she wrote:

> And in the evening, when I lie in bed and end my prayers with the words, "I thank you, God, for all that is good and dear and beautiful," I am filled with joy. Then I think about "the good" of going into hiding, of my health and with my whole being of the "dearness" of Peter [her friend] . . . and of "the beauty" which exists in the world. . . .
>
> I don't think then of all the misery, but of the beauty that still remains. . . . Look at these things, then you find yourself again, and God, and then you regain your bal-ance.
>
> And whoever is happy will make others happy too. He who has courage and faith will never perish in misery! (*Anne Frank,* page 184)

Like her Jewish ancestors singing psalms of thanks, Anne experienced life as a gift from God. She understood the essential truth of what Christians call the paschal mystery: that life will be victorious over death. She would not have expressed it in the Christian terms of Saint Paul, but she would probably have shared the spirit of his words to the Corinthians:

> We know that the one who raised the Lord Jesus will raise us also with Jesus, and will bring us with you into his presence. Yes, everything is for your sake, so that grace, as it extends to more and more people, may increase thanksgiving, to the glory of God. (2 Corinthians 4:14–15)

6

JOURNAL WRITING

A CONVERSATION WITH GOD

When we live prayerfully, we find many ways to respond to God's presence. In this chapter we will take a look at the value of a personal journal as a way of maintaining a conversation with God and as a means of helping us to better understand ourselves.

A Journal: Writing About One's Life

The English word *journal* has been adopted directly from the French word that translates as "daily." People keep personal journals so that they have a written record of their experiences, ideas, and reflections on their life and on the world around them.

People have kept personal journals throughout history. In fact, journals that have survived from years and centuries gone by have been important sources of information for historians, sociologists, and others who study the past. Anne Frank's diary has provided much insight into the experience of a persecuted Jewish family during World War II. More recently, a young victim of the chaos of the war in Bosnia-Herzegovina kept a journal, published in English in 1994 as *Zlata's Diary: A Child's Life in Sarajevo*. Zlata's own account gave the world a unique understanding of the suffering caused by war.

Stimulating Conversation

Just as the personal journals of others are useful tools for students of history, our own journals can be tools for understanding ourselves, our experiences, and our relationships. Keeping a journal is like holding an extended and stimulating conversation.

> **In companionship and conversation, we learn a lot about ourselves.**

As part of our human nature, we desire, even yearn, to communicate with others, and one basic method of communication is conversation. When we converse, we keep someone company. Company comes from two Latin words, *com* and *panis,* which mean "with" and "bread." When we converse with someone, we nurture each other like two people sharing bread, the most basic of foods.

In conversation, we learn from one another. We gain information. Sometimes the most important information we gain has to do with ourselves. In fact, our self-image, for better and for worse, is developed from the feedback or reactions we receive from other people. Much of that feedback comes through conversations.

When we talk with colleagues, for example, we can learn a lot about ourselves. Our conversations might be about simple everyday matters, but in the midst of them we discover new things about one another. Consider Bill, who gave an oral report for his management team. He had worked hard to prepare but was still very nervous; he was afraid he would forget something or that everyone would notice his hands trembling. After the presentation, at lunch, another member of the team commented: "I liked your report. You're easy to listen to, and you were well prepared. Your presentation will make our next quarter go more smoothly." Bill admitted that he had been quite anxious about it, and the coworker said, "I couldn't tell, and I was right across from you." In this brief conversation, Bill learned something about himself and gained new confidence in his ability as a public presenter.

Why Keep a Journal?

Keeping a journal enables us to carry on a special kind of conversation—a conversation with ourselves. In this exchange we are free to reflect on our experiences and learn from them. What we usually learn is something about ourselves. In addition, the journal provides the opportunity to play with new ideas and work through some of our current difficulties.

Learning About and Loving Oneself

One explanation of why people keep a journal comes from Anne Frank's diary: "I want to write, but more than that, I want to bring out all kinds of things that lie buried deep in my heart" (*Anne Frank,* page 12).

As we write, it is almost inevitable that we will touch the "things that lie buried" in our heart. We will encounter who we really are.

This reason for writing is echoed by other authors. The award-winning playwright Edward Albee said: "Writing has got to be an act of discovery. . . . I write to find out what I'm thinking about" (Charles R. Cooper and Lee Odell, editors, *Research on Composing,* page 101). The novelist James Baldwin approached writing in this way: "You go into a book and you're in the dark, really. You go in with a certain fear and trembling. You know one thing. You know you will not be the same person when this voyage is over. But you don't know what's going to happen to you between getting on the boat and stepping off" (page 101). Robert Frost said, "For me the initial delight is in the surprise of remembering something I didn't know I knew" (page 101). Poet Adrienne Rich shared a similar discovery: "Poems are like dreams; you put into them what you don't know you know" (page 103). Writing is a voyage of discovering ourselves.

One possible result of greater self-knowledge is that we will begin to like ourselves more. We will better recognize our own talents and gifts and skills. We will become more accepting of our feelings, even negative ones. By being more honest with ourselves, we will recognize our limitations and strengths and develop a greater satisfaction with who we are. And we will see more clearly that love of ourselves is the strongest basis we have for loving others.

A Place to Work Things Through

Many people keep a journal for working out problems. Recall some conflict that you have had. Maybe you argued with your spouse or child. Maybe you received a low evaluation on a project that you thought represented your best effort. When a tangle of emotions and ideas throws us into confusion, we just cannot seem to get our head clear or to gain a fresh perspective.

Writing in a journal can help. Writing helps us focus on various aspects of any experience. Putting things down on a page first of all enables us to release pent-up emotions and reactions. This in itself can be valuable and can help us get perspective. Scattered fragments of experience gain a concrete, objective form on paper. When we have written down all the pieces, we can review the whole experience and sort it out, which helps us to better understand it.

For example, when Francis received an offer for a new and better position in a large city in another area of the country, he and his wife, Eleanor, both wrote in their journals about the optional move, and then discussed the issue thoroughly with each other before they came to a decision that would affect the whole family. Initially they each felt exhilarated and anxious in the face of the new possibilities. To see the situation more clearly, they each sat down with a journal and began to write. They recorded both the advantages and disadvantages of the new situation, and the advantages and disadvantages of the present situation.

Doing this did not make Francis and Eleanor's decision easier or less painful, but it did allow them to make some sense of the complex emotions they were experiencing and to get an idea of which issues were most important. By putting their experiences on paper, they could sort through all the elements and see them from new perspectives.

Prayer and the Journal

If prayer is our awareness of and response to God's presence in our life, what part does keeping a journal play in prayer? When we use our journal prayerfully, we are actually taking on God as our partner in conversation. By sharing from the heart in this way, we are relating with God. Through the journal, our life and our experience become the starting point for our prayer.

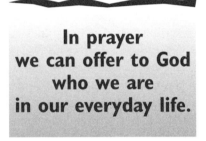

**In prayer
we can offer to God
who we are
in our everyday life.**

Praying Our Experiences

God created all things. So God cannot be surprised by anything; God has seen it all. Humans may be surprised, but not God. To us who believe that God dwells everywhere and in all things, God is here and now, in all that we say and think and do. It is a quite natural thing to share with God about our everyday realities. Also, the only thing we as human beings have to offer back to God is ourselves, expressing to God who we are.

So when we pray, converse, or keep company with God, whether in our heart or on paper in a journal, we need not formulate fancy prose or say the perfect words. God wants conversation that concerns who we really are. In his book *Praying Our Experiences,* Joseph F. Schmidt explains his title in this way:

> By *praying* I mean offering in honesty and surrender the reality of myself and my life history to the Lord. . . .
> By ***praying our experiences,*** then, I mean . . . getting in touch with who I am as the person who has had an experience, and offering that *who* to God through reflection on that experience. (Boldface added; pages 7–8)

This offering of our experience, of who we are, is the gift we can give to God. This type of giving is much like that between two friends. Often the most precious gifts friends exchange are something of themselves: listening, sharing concerns, being empathetic, and so on.

So when we converse with God in prayer, we can simply tell God of our everyday life. Praying this way can be as revealing as talking with our best friends, and even more so. After all, even with our best friends we tend to omit some topics or information. With God, who knows all, we can open ourselves completely.

When we pray our experiences, all the elements of our life come into play as we respond to God's presence. Our particular historical, family, and cultural situation—that is, the details of our life—have an important place in the ongoing development of our relationship with God. So when we reflect on our everyday realities, whether in thought, in conversation, or in a journal, it makes sense to consciously bring God into the process.

God Revealed in the Everyday

God seldom shows up in a burst of thunder or in a miraculous apparition. Instead human beings encounter God in the midst of day-to-day life, with all its positive and negative elements. Really paying attention to people and events can be a way of listening to God. For instance, if I find that I am constantly irritated with my friends, a bit of reflection might help me figure out what God is trying to communicate to me. Perhaps my irritation is God's way of saying to me: "Time to look deeper! Maybe you are ready to grow more, and your friends are not. Maybe you're looking for something different in friendships than you used to." On the other hand, God may be asking me to take a deeper look at myself, at my own tendency to judge people harshly.

To pray our experiences also implies that we believe that God actually does reside deep within us. The great spiritual writers believed this. For example, Saint Teresa of Ávila compared the soul to an "interior castle" with many rooms:

> Well, let us consider that this castle has . . . many dwelling places: some up above, others down below, others to the sides; and in the center and middle is the main dwelling place where the very secret exchanges between God and the soul take place. (Otilio Rodriguez and Kieran Kavanaugh, translators, *The Collected Works of St. Teresa of Ávila*, volume 2, page 284)

Teresa acknowledged that most of the time our spirit wanders in places other than the interior room where we converse with God. However, she never doubted that God dwells within us, even if we do not visit with God very often.

Saint Teresa gained her assurance that God dwells within from the words of Jesus that promised that the Holy Spirit would dwell with us (John 14:5–18). Saint Paul wrote that "God's love has been poured into our hearts through the Holy Spirit that has been given to us" (Romans 5:5). So when we listen to what our heart speaks in all honesty, we can encounter God there.

Consequently, when we bring our experiences to prayer, we seek the hand of God in those experiences. We ask God to show us what God is offering in those events. Even a painful occurrence can nourish our spirit and call us to be fully alive if we ask the right questions about it: Why am I hurt by this experience? What does it tell me about the way I live my life? What can I learn about relating to other people from this experience? Does this event teach me about my priorities? Is this event calling me to depend more on God's love and less on my own control of things?

By reflecting on the joyful and the painful parts of life, we can grow in self-knowledge. We become "bigger" selves and, therefore, have more to offer back to God. We certainly have more to talk about.

Keeping a Journal

For journal writing to be meaningful, a sincere attitude is important. We need to approach the experience of keeping a journal, determined to be honest. This means desiring to confront all sides of who we are. It also means wanting to grow in our relationships with other people and with God.

If you are skeptical about the value of keeping a journal, you are not alone. But give it a try. If you are open to what you might learn from the experience, keeping a journal will be at least interesting, perhaps even amazingly revealing.

Practical Suggestions

1. **Write in your journal daily or at least often and regularly.** Writing every day pushes you to spend even a few minutes conversing with your soul and with God, focusing on the shape of your life.

2. **Decide what you will do about sharing the contents of your journal with others.** Be careful of writing for an audience other than yourself and God. You may want to keep your journal entirely private, to encourage total honesty.

3. **Use a spacious notebook.** Write in a notebook with plenty of space to expand on your thoughts and feelings. You may want to paste in pictures or draw in it, so you need room. And since a journal is also a record, with a notebook you will have all your entries bound together for easy reference. (As an alternative, you may prefer writing on a computer.)

4. **Use a pen.** Pencil smudges may make future references to your journal difficult. You might have some colored pens handy, too—just in case you get an urge to draw or decorate.

5. **Date all your entries.** This practice helps you find entries if you wish to later.

6. **Before you begin writing, relax.** Relaxing your body and taking some deep breaths can clear the mind and encourage words to flow.

7. **Write, write, write.** Journal writers do not need to worry about correct grammar, spelling, punctuation, margins, and so on. Be spontaneous. Censoring or fretting over correctness will cramp your style. Just write. And then write some more.

8. **Write about anything.** Many suggestions about topics and methods will be given later in this chapter, but anything can be included in your journal. The essential feature of your writing should be that it is honest, spontaneous conversation.

9. **Warning: If having your name and address on the journal makes you hesitant about being honest, leave them off.**

10. **Keep your journal in a safe place, even under lock and key.** Your journal and its contents belong to you, and no one has a right to read it unless you give him or her that privilege.

Basic Techniques

The basic technique for keeping a journal, again, is just to write, and then write some more. At times, however, you may need help getting started or need direction for dealing with a particular type of situation. Several techniques can be used on a regular basis or simply as you need them.

Freewriting

Freewriting means exactly that: writing freely and spontaneously whatever comes to mind, letting ideas and feelings flow out unchecked. When freewriting, try to write continuously, hardly lifting pen from paper. If you get stuck, write some word or phrase over and over until something else comes to mind.

Try to take a playful attitude toward this sort of journal writing. Chances are you will uncover some surprises, and that is the point of freewriting. After freewriting you may decide to examine one of the surprises further, using another journal-writing technique.

Composing Unsent Letters

If you have ever been furious with someone but knew you could not tell the person of your anger directly, or if you have ever fallen madly in love but were afraid to express your feelings out loud, then you probably can understand the value of writing a letter that will not be sent. Sometimes just the exercise of writing can help us get rid of our anger or name our love.

Writing unsent letters in our journal gives us a chance to say anything to anyone, even God. Also, writing unsent letters gives us a sense of having an audience to communicate with. Many of us find writing to a person easier than just writing to a blank sheet of paper. Zlata of Sarajevo called her diary Mimmy. Alice Walker's moving novel *The Color Purple* consisted largely of unsent letters to God written by the main character, Celie, an abused, poor black woman.

You can write an unsent letter to anyone whom you wish to tell things that you cannot or should not say directly. It might also be useful to consider how you could change the letter if you really did intend to send it.

Unsent letters can also be written to someone to whom you have not had a chance to express your thoughts and feelings—for example, someone who has died.

Writing Dialog

Even when we do freewriting, a dialog is going on inside us. We respond to some question buzzing around in our mind. The question might be, What was I thinking about when I did that? or, How am I really feeling about this? In any case, most writing reacts to a question or a series of internal statements.

Sometimes, stating the questions explicitly and then answering them can help us understand what we are thinking about and feeling. When we write both the questions and our answers, we are engaging in a dialog. All sorts of insights can result. We begin to see two sides of an issue. We take the part of someone else and view the matter at hand from her or his point of view. In short, we gain various perspectives.

Effective dialog writing demands that we be willing to take on two sides of an issue. When you write dialog, jot down whatever first comes to mind. Do not censor any comment or structure the dialog. As in freewriting and in composing unsent letters, let the words flow. Do not stop to analyze what is going on—that can come later, during a period of reflection.

Helpful dialog partners might be other people, God, Jesus, the Holy Spirit, your body, your emotions. Here is a sample dialog in which Linda talks to her anger:

Linda: I lost it again with Greg. Why do I get so angry?

Anger: Hey, maybe you have a right to be angry!

Linda: I don't get it. I'm not supposed to be angry. He gets so upset. I'm supposed to be nice.

Anger: Is he nice to you? I mean, he gets pretty bullying and always wants to make all the decisions, even though he isn't willing to live with the consequences. He orders you around and is never sensitive to your needs or preferences. Do you like that?

Linda: No, I hate it. It's driving me crazy.

Anger: So maybe it's okay to be angry, and maybe you should let him know it. You have a right to be involved in your life together, don't you?

Prayer Journal Writing

Many people write daily prayers to God as a way of keeping company with the Creator. Numerous types of prayers can be included in your journal: you can ask God for help or strength, express sorrow to God about something, reflect on scriptural passages, give thanks and praise, and so on. However, a prayer journal does not have to be limited to forms of prayer such as these—prayers can be any expression of what you want to say to God.

Daily Journal Writing

Asking yourself three basic questions can lead you into daily journal writing:

◆ What happened today?

◆ How did I feel about these experiences?

◆ What did I learn from what happened?

From a Christian perspective, God works in all our life events. By looking for insights through these three questions, you may find new ways of living fully.

Conversing with the Past

To arrive at some understanding of the present, we need to look at the past. Our beliefs and behaviors have been shaped by our past experience of ourselves, our relationships, the world, and God. Keeping a journal can help us look back at some areas of our past as we try to make sense of the present and plan for the future.

Events

One method for exploring the past is to brainstorm, in your journal, a list of all the important events of your personal history—from your earliest memories to your most recent significant moments. What is considered an important event? Anything that has special meaning for you; you be the judge. It might be an accident, an award, meeting a great friend, a crisis in your family, a significant accomplishment, a revealing conversation. Be as thorough as possible in making your list.

When you have finished the list, read it over slowly. Select one event from the first third of your life, one from the second third of your life, one from the last third of your life, and one from the past year. Then imagine that you are explaining to a good friend why each event was important to you. In writing tell how each event has made you the person you are.

Decisions

A second method for conversing with the past is to look at some of your most important decisions. We shape our character by the decisions we make over the course of our life. In your journal list as many key decisions as you can think of. Maybe you decided to quit smoking. Maybe you decided to change careers. Maybe you decided to become a parent.

As in writing about important events, select a significant decision you made in each third of your life and in the last year. For each decision write a dialog with yourself at the age you made the decision. Start by asking why you made the decision. Find out what was involved and what the effects have been. Tell that younger self how that decision is still influencing you.

> **A significant moment in our past may be the focus of an imaginary dialog.**

People

A final method for conversing with the past is to imagine that you have invited the five most influential people in your life to dinner. Draw an oval tabletop and place mats for six people. Write your name at one of the end seats at the table. Then, at the remaining seats, write in the names of your five mentors, guides, or significant influences; they may be relatives, parents, friends, national figures, teachers—any persons who have had a powerful effect on shaping your character.

Now write out a dinner conversation in which each of these persons talks about you, and you say what these persons mean to you or how they influenced you. For an interesting variation, have some of your "dinner guests" talk to one another in your journal.

Conversing with the Present

Considering the past can help us to learn about ourselves in the present, but it would be a mistake to get stuck in the past and not live fully now. So much happens from day to day that sometimes life seems to flash by in a blur. Many revealing moments may be lost in the rush of events. We need to stay in touch with the present.

The Facts of Your Life

So where are you now? Who are you? What is important to you? Through your journal you can converse with the present. One way to approach this is to list all the facts of your life as you are living it right now. For example:

Current Conditions of My Life

1. I have one more year with my children living at home, and I don't know what to do with my energies and daily routine once they are gone.
2. My car insurance went up after an accident, so I may have to budget differently.
3. I've been looking for a different job because I'm getting co-opted into unethical financial behavior in my workplace.

Decisions

You can also make a list of at least five significant decisions you face right now. Next to each decision, write a brief description of what is at stake, what you are thinking with regard to the decision, and how you feel about the decision. You might even write a dialog in which all the perspectives involved in a particular decision are given a voice and a chance to express their views.

Blessings and Fears

The freewriting technique offers opportunities to look spontaneously at how you perceive your own gifts, blessings, loves, and fears. Writing freely whatever comes to mind, complete each of the following statements as well as you can:

◆ I have been given many blessings, like . . .
◆ The gifts I would like to give to the world today are . . .
◆ Love has given me . . .
◆ I become fearful or anxious when I think of . . .

Friends and Enemies

In daily life your friends are likely very important to you. In your journal write a definition of the word *friend*. Then list all the people who are your friends right now, leaving a space below each name. In the space for each name, answer these questions:

◆ What holds our friendship together?
◆ What does this friendship give me?

◆ What do I give to this friendship?

◆ How could our relationship be better?

You can also take this approach to writing about people you think of as your enemies. Answer these questions:

◆ What started the ill will between us?

◆ How have I contributed to the continuing hostility?

◆ How could we change this tense situation?

Another technique for reflecting on a strained relationship is to write an imaginary dialog with the other person. Begin with one of you saying, "How come we're enemies?"

Family

When you hear the word *family,* what does it mean for you? Based on your definition, list the names of the people you consider as your family. Then complete the following statements:

◆ To my family, I contribute . . .

◆ My family gives me . . .

◆ From my family, I need more . . .

Faith and Religion

Writing in a journal can be a religious or spiritual activity whether or not the things we write about have God or religion as their focus. But we can also reflect on themes that are specifically religious. Here are some explicitly religious statements:

◆ The eight deepest desires of my heart are . . .

◆ I experience God right now in . . .

◆ When I think of the word *holy,* I . . .

◆ When I consider Jesus, I . . .

◆ For me right now, going to church means . . .

◆ If I want to meet God, I . . .

◆ My deepest doubts in regard to God and religion are . . .

You might want to complete these statements in your journal. Or you might write a dialog with God, beginning with your asking a question that seems important to you, such as, "Why do you seem so far away from me, God?"

Conversing with the Future

A journal can be an ideal place to dream about and plan for the future. Dreams give zest and purpose to life, and we need plans to realize how to make our dreams reality. Dreams and plans help us shape our present decisions and actions.

Journal writing about the future may be compared to writing science fiction: we project into the future based on what we know now, and create a story for that future.

Wish Lists

One way to approach the future in your journal is to list as quickly as you can the dreams you have for your future; include all your dreams, even if they seem silly or trivial.

When you have finished your list, ponder it and pick one dream or combination of dreams that seems to give you a lot of energy. Using all the powers of your imagination, write a thorough description of this big dream; be as complete as possible.

You might want to expand on this by writing down ten decisions that you will have to make in order to bring your dream to reality.

God's Place

It is also good to think about the future in terms of your relationship with God. One way to start this kind of reflection is to complete the following statements in your journal:

◆ In the future I want God to . . .
◆ In terms of my future, I think God wants me to . . .

Living the Questions

This chapter began with a discussion of conversation. In human relationships and in our relationship with God, conversations allow us to make an offer of ourselves. By engaging in conversation, we also learn about ourselves. Through this process we grow; we develop more and more to bring to our conversations—and to our relationships.

By keeping a journal, we carry on a conversation with ourselves and with God. We have a chance to express our feelings, ponder, work things through, pray, heal within, decide, dream, and plan. A journal is a place where many things can happen, including our developing an awareness of God and responding more fully to the presence of God. As a result, a journal can be a great tool for growing inside, so that we may build a better world outside.

A journal is a place where we can ask a lot of questions, yet we do not need to have all the "right" answers. Sometimes just the process of wrestling with the questions is enough to enable us to grow. A poet of the early twentieth century, Rainer Maria Rilke, once wrote about this to a young man. His advice to the youth is useful for anyone who takes seriously his or her own life and wants to reflect in writing on that life:

> Be patient toward all that is unsolved in your heart and . . . try to love the *questions themselves*. . . . Do not now seek the answers, which cannot be given you because you would not be able to live them. And the point is, to live everything. *Live* the questions now. Perhaps you will then gradually, without noticing it, live along some distant day into the answer. (*Letters to a Young Poet,* page 35)

7

MEDITATION

DWELLING ON THE MYSTERY OF GOD

People experience a hunger for meditation, even if they do not know what to name the hunger. The hunger might begin with an uneasy sense that life is somehow empty. It might start with a feeling of being so pushed and pulled that they desperately want to say: "Time out! Give me space and quiet!" The need for meditation might even come from a coach telling an athlete, "You have to learn to concentrate."

The Hunger for Meditation

Poetry often expresses the hunger for meditation and the search for silence and equilibrium.

Word-Filled Days

Out of name-filled days,
Traffic jams,
And neon signs at night,
I search for silence.

Find it—in moments
Stolen out of time
In quiet seclusion
Of a moving car
An emptied classroom,
Waiting for the bells.
Anonymity
Of subway train!
Or doctor's waiting room.

Lonely in crowds,
Companioned by my problems,
I need withdrawal
To briefly, reflectively
Pray myself back
Into the place
Where I belong;
Guided, rejoicing
To celebrate the day

(Anita Wheatcroft,
in Carl Koch, editor, *Womenpsalms,* page 67)

A Common Human Experience

Meditation is a timeless and universal human practice, a natural and common part of human life. People desire to meditate and even meditate often without knowing it. Meditation is also a discipline demanding constant effort, long practice, and fervent desire. Hindu gurus, Catholic hermits, Muslim Sufis, Buddhist monks, and American Indian shamans spend years practicing meditation.

What exactly is meditation? All definitions come back to a central theme: meditation is pondering, attending, dwelling upon, or paying attention to. It is more than a technique to focus our attention for discrete time periods of, say, fifteen minutes. It is a practice that helps us to live mindfully or consciously in all of life, aware of what is right before us, rather than scattered and distracted.

We need to learn meditation because life swirls around us at dizzying speed. For example, you wake up in the morning, make sure everyone has breakfast, and move on to the next activity with your eye on the clock. During the morning you have things to attend to, telephone calls to make, activities to supervise. Later in the day, you have meals to prepare, after-school events to organize, meetings to attend, and so on. Taking time out in the midst of our day to quiet ourselves within and to ponder can benefit us all.

Christian Meditation

Christian meditation builds on the usual quieting and centering techniques of meditation and goes beyond them. It uses the attentiveness and mindfulness of ordinary meditation to focus on God and the mystery of God's love for us as given to us in Jesus. Christian meditation clears a path within us so that we can experience union with God in Jesus Christ.

In a reflection on her life, Karen DeFilippis recounts her middle-of-the-night experiences.

> I've always treasured 2:00 a.m. feedings. It seemed to be the only time that I got to hold my baby without having to divide my time between the other children. In the middle of the night, the two-year-old that was always eager to plant sticky peanut-butter kisses on the nursing baby was now sound asleep, scrubbed squeaky clean and tucked between fresh sheets. The four-year-old who always brought me his favorite book at precisely the same moment that the baby needed to be fed was now safe and sound asleep in dreams, with his books scattered on the floor all around him. Even my considerate husband, who shared with me all the details of his business transactions of the day, was now making sounds of contented, deep sleep. And so I am alone with our baby. This is my time to recapture the intimacy we shared when only I knew the inner stirrings of

the child nestled deep within my womb. Now this precious infant belongs to everyone, and I must claim my intimate moments at two o'clock in the morning.

One night as I sat in the dark of my living room holding the baby that had fallen asleep at my breast, I marveled at the gift of life. This gift of life *given to me.* This child, so fragile, so dependent, is loved unconditionally simply because he exists. He grew in my womb and was brought forth in living water, making me so vulnerable, making me see life brand new all over again. I know that if a hair were brushed to the wrong side, I would know it. If he were to get hurt I would feel the pain. To love so much is to allow myself to be unbelievably vulnerable.

Somewhere in my wonderings at 2:00 a.m., I began a dialog with God. I knew in my head that God's love was even more perfect than mine, but I couldn't understand it in my heart. How could there be a more perfect love than that of parents for their child? Two o'clock became a sacramental moment, for I was able to see that the child asleep in my lap was a perfect container for God's love. To look at the face of God and know God's love would be too awesome for me to handle. In the image of my child I could safely encounter the unconditional love of God.

The early morning feeding and the baby became the sacred time and place in which I could connect with God. At some point I became acutely aware of God's love enveloping me. I became the baby lying in the lap of God. I felt the presence of a God who feels my pain and counts the hairs on my head. I was aware of being intimately connected to God, my Creator. The union was as intimate as the connection between me and the child that grew in my womb. In the dark of my living room I knew what it was like to live in the womb of God. I felt the nurturing power of God's love pulsing through me. I knew that the source of all my love was God. At the 2:00 a.m. feeding, I was being fed. Sometime between the dark of night and the light of day I was called by name, and I came to know what it means to be a daughter of God. ("Living in the Womb of God" in Koch, editor, *Womenpsalms,* pages 98–99)

Karen's description of this moment accurately portrays what happens in meditation. Our attention is focused. We often become more relaxed and calm. Our thoughts and feelings move into deeper dimensions of life and faith. As a believer in God, Karen discovers God and appreciates the divine mystery in this living and life-giving moment.

The Benefits of Meditation

Meditation, though a common human experience, takes discipline to learn. It does not come automatically, but must be practiced with patience. For those willing to put in the time and disciplined effort, not expecting quick results, the benefits are many.

Being on Intimate Terms with God

For thousands of years, members of all religious traditions have understood the benefits of meditation. In all religions meditation plays an essential role in developing the relationship between the person and the Holy—no matter what the Holy is called. Buddhists meditate to empty the mind of desire so that enlightenment might have a place to enter. Muslims ponder their sacred scriptures, the Qur'an, to comprehend the will of Allah (the One God). Christian mystics meditate upon the wonders of God's revelations in nature, in the Bible, and in their experience of Jesus.

Finding Balance in Life

When life goes sour, when everything seems out of order, meditation brings us back to an awareness of God's abiding presence and the many great—even if simple—miracles of the life God has given us. The writer of Psalm 77 moans about all the disasters in his life and even doubts that God really cares about him, but then he says:

> I will call to mind the deeds of the LORD;
> > I will remember your wonders of old.
> I will meditate on all your work,
> > and muse on your mighty deeds.

(Verses 11–12)

Through meditation the Psalmist puts life back into perspective, saying gratefully, "What god is so great as our God?" (verse 13).

Healing

Although the great religions have always known the healing effects of meditation, modern medicine and psychology have only recently come to acknowledge them. Many studies have shown that meditation reduces stress. Serious stress can elevate blood pressure, increase the incidence of heart attack, and contribute to a host of other diseases and chronic illnesses. The medical profession is even beginning to recognize the healing and curative effects of meditation for cancer patients.

Living Life to the Full

Meditation places us in the present and puts us in the habit of paying attention to what is right in front of us. It gives us a deeper experience of our own life. A medical expert who teaches meditation to sufferers of chronic pain and stress-related medical disorders says that given a meditation exercise to do, patients quickly find out they are not used to focusing on the present, such as noticing what they are eating. Then, he says,

> it's a very short jump to realize that you may actually not be in touch with many of the moments of your life, because you're so busy rushing someplace else that you aren't in the present moment. Your life is the sum of your present moments, so if you're missing lots of them, you may actually miss much of your children's infancy and youth, or beautiful sunsets, or the beauty of your own body. You may be tuning out all sorts of inner and outer experiences simply because you're too preoccupied with where you want to get, what you want to have happen, and what you don't want to happen. (Jon Kabat-Zinn, quoted in Bill Moyers, *Healing and the Mind*, page 117)

Life can pass us by if we are not "all there."

The great Russian writer Leo Tolstoy once told a story about a hermit who knew the importance of living in the present:

> Tolstoy, in his famous *Twenty-Three Tales,* devotes the final one to describing a king who is in search of an answer to three questions: How can I learn to do the right thing at the right time? Whose advice can I trust? And what things are most important and require my first attention?
>
> Disguised in simple clothes, the king visited a hermit deep in the wood and asked him his three questions. Getting no answer but finding the frail hermit on the verge of collapse [from the exertion of working in the garden], the king took over the hermit's spade and finished digging his garden. At sunset a bearded man staggered in with a terrible bleeding stomach wound, dealt him by one of the king's bodyguards who were scattered through the forest to protect him. The king washed the wound, bandaged it with a towel and handkerchief, and kept changing the bandages until the flow of blood stopped and the man could be carried into the hut. The king slept the night on the threshold of the hut and when morning came, found the bearded man confessing that he had lain in wait for the king's return from the hermit's hut, having sworn to kill him for a judgment the king had once given against him. He begged the king's forgiveness and pledged to serve him. The king, promising to send his own physician to attend him, rose to go but again put his questions to the hermit, complaining that he had still received no answer to them.
>
> **We may let life pass us by if we are not "all there."**
>
> The hermit insisted that the king had twice received his answers on the previous day: When the king appeared on the previous afternoon, the hermit in his weakness did not see how he could finish digging his garden, and the king had relieved him. This was the right thing at the right time and the most important to be done—for had he returned through the wood at that time, his enemy would have killed him. When the wound-

ed man appeared, stanching his blood and relieving him was the right thing at the right time and made a friend of an enemy. "Remember then," added the hermit, "there is only one time that is important. Now!" And further, "The most necessary man is he with whom you are . . . and the most important thing is to do him good, because for that purpose alone was man sent into this life!" (Douglas V. Steere, *On Being Present Where You Are,* pages 12–13)

A habit of meditating teaches us to focus on what is right before us so that we do not go through life missing the obvious, even missing out on life itself. Meditation helps us live to the full.

Approaching Meditation

No one way of meditating fits everyone. Because of variations in personality, we each need to find a way of meditating that is best for us. Some people try to empty their mind of all thoughts. Others meditate on biblical passages or other sacred texts (see chapter 8, which covers meditation on the Scriptures). In some traditions of meditation, people chant sacred words out loud or repeat a word in harmony with their breathing in the silence of their mind. Some people meditate by writing in their journal (see chapter 6). There are eating meditations, walking meditations, and even meditations with dance or other body movement. In short, to learn our own way or ways, we need to try various methods of dwelling on, pondering, and attending to God.

Common Features

Certain common features of all the various methods will help us meditate more effectively.

Openness to the Power of Meditation

As with all forms of prayer, meditation can open your mind and broaden your vision. Be open to new ways of seeing God, other people, and yourself. All of life is filled with God's presence. As you prepare to meditate, remind yourself that God is present and that dwelling with God for these moments can be a powerful experience.

A Quiet Space

When two friends want to talk seriously, they go to a quiet park or room, not a rock concert or an overly crowded restaurant. Meditation, too, requires space and quiet. Although any place may work, some locations aid meditation more than others.

Ideally, find a quiet room, a natural setting, or a chapel for meditation. If you can meditate in a spot regularly, create a prayerful atmosphere with candles, meditative music, an open Bible, a crucifix.

If privacy and silence are not possible, create a quiet, safe place within yourself, perhaps while riding to or from work on a bus or subway, while waiting for someone, or whenever you have a chance. Do the best you can, knowing that a loving God is present everywhere.

A Regular Time

Some people can barely open their eyes in the morning, whereas other people have run out of steam by the time supper is done. People who have a serious desire to meditate need to find some regular time to do so that fits their biological clock as well as the rhythm of their daily activities.

Prayerful Posture

The best posture for meditation also varies from person to person, but ideally it should allow for free circulation of your blood—so that your arms or legs do not go to sleep—and should help you stay alert but comfortable. Wearing comfortable clothes will allow freedom of movement for finding and maintaining the best body position.

Here are several postures used for meditation:

- Kneeling with the back straight and the hands folded in front of the body, resting on something—a chair, a couch, a pew—to give support and balance
- Kneeling with the body relaxed and the buttocks resting on the heels of the feet, the back straight, the head upright, and the hands resting on the thighs
- Sitting in a firm, straight-backed chair, the upper body erect, the feet together and placed firmly on the floor, the hands gently resting on the lap (Some people prefer sitting on the edge of the chair.)

- Reclining on the floor, the body straight, the legs uncrossed, and the hands in a relaxed position (Some people support their knees with a pillow underneath them.)
- Sitting on the floor, the legs folded and the back straight, the hands resting on the knees (Some people lean against a wall with a pillow against their spine.)

◆ Try each posture in the above list to find the one that best suits you.

Dealing with Our Wandering Mind

As we try to pay attention or ponder, our mind naturally tends to wander all over. Our body may be sitting erect in a straight-backed chair, but our mind is arguing with our colleagues, stewing about a parking ticket, or musing about the children. These distractions take us out of the present; they lead us away from meditation. Paradoxically, if we try to push distractions away or force them out of our mind, we end up paying even more attention to them.

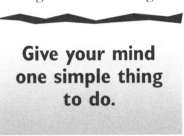

Give your mind one simple thing to do.

One way of handling distractions is to give the mind a simple thing to do, like the task this master gave his restless elephant:

> While carrying its master through the narrow streets of a village, the elephant with its wandering trunk was constantly getting into trouble. Swaying one way, it would grab a bunch of bananas from a fruit stand and, in a single gulp, put its master in debt to the vendor. Sometimes it would reach for a peeled coconut on the other side. Left to its own instincts, the elephant would never stop moving its trunk to and fro and getting into mischief.
>
> Given the elephant's innocence and loyalty to its master, the difficulty was overcome in a simple manner. The wise master gave the elephant a bamboo shaft to hold with its trunk. Without understanding why, the elephant obediently held the shaft high and steady as it walked through the village. In faithfully performing this simple task, the elephant was freed from being tempted by all the attractions along the path.

Most forms of meditation operate on the same principle that the elephant's master used. Whether we gaze at a candle, pay attention to our breathing, repeat a sacred word, or dwell on a scriptural verse, the underlying idea is the same: we give our mind one simple thing to do, and it will be freed from countless other distractions and begin to quiet itself. Eventually the simple task may be forgotten, and our mind may be still and focused. If distractions start buzzing around again, we simply take up the simple task again until the distractions leave.

We should not become anxious, stressed, or angry at our distractions. They are natural. However, we do not function at our best with our thoughts zooming all over. Meditation helps to gently train our mind to pay attention. To live mindfully or consciously demands intentness. Great golfers know that they excel because they are able to concentrate on what they are doing. If they are thinking about how many strokes they are behind or about the prize money, they will likely miss the crucial putt or hook the drive that will get them on the green. To do any task well, to love well, demands being completely attentive and focused on the present moment.

Ways of Meditating

Each of the following meditations provides a different experience. All may be repeated with variations that you may add over time. Before you begin any of them, prepare your prayer place and assume your prayer posture.

Exercises of Simple Awareness

God created all of life and declared that it "was very good" (Genesis 1:31). One way of praising the Creator is to pay attention to, wonder at, and appreciate creation. By meditating in simple awareness of ourselves and the world, we give praise to God, but we also learn to focus our attention.

Nature Meditation
Find an item in nature that reminds you of God the Creator and bring the object to your place of prayer. Or, if possible, find a spot in a park, in your yard, or at a window from which you can observe

some wonder of nature. The act of looking for the item or place can be meditative in itself.

When you have found the natural object or your special spot, recall that God the Creator is with you. Then just gaze at this piece of creation. Study its texture, its shape, its color, and so on. If you start thinking of something else, just focus on the object again.

After this time of pondering, speak words of thanks to God for the marvelous gifts to be found in creation.

The Sounds of Silence

In focusing on the sounds of silence, you may learn to accept noises as a backdrop for meditation rather than as distractions. You will also have time to pay attention to the gift of hearing.

Begin the meditation by closing your eyes, quieting yourself, and steadying your breathing. Relax your body. Remember that God is present with you and in you. Plug your ears with your thumbs and place the palms of your hands over your closed eyes. The only sound you will likely hear is that of your own breathing. Listen to that sound.

After taking ten full breaths in this position, gently remove your hands from your face and rest them on your lap. Keep your eyes closed. Now listen to all the sounds that surround you—within the room, throughout the house, outdoors—every sound. Identify each sound in terms of its source and its distance from you—the creak of a stair in the hallway ten feet away, the roar of a passing truck on the highway at the end of the block.

Finally, recognize that all sounds, both in their origins and in your ability to hear them, are reflections of the creative and sustaining power of God. Thank God for the sounds and for your gift of hearing. Allow yourself to rest peacefully in the midst of the sounds.

(This exercise is based on one by Anthony de Mello, in *Sadhana, a Way to God*, pages 47–49.)

Following Your Breath

Some religious traditions make breathing a central practice of meditation. Deep breathing releases stress and concentrates our attention. A period of deep breathing at the start of every meditation can prepare us to be more focused and calm.

Sitting upright and quiet, become aware of your breathing. Do not try to control or analyze the process of respiration; simply become conscious of it.

Follow your breathing carefully. Slowly inhale through your nostrils and let the air flow all the way to the bottom of your diaphragm, filling your lungs completely. Then slowly and gently exhale through your mouth. Again, inhale deeply and exhale slowly. Do this ten times.

As you continue to breathe deeply, imagine that each time you inhale you are filling yourself more and more with God's peace. Imagine as well that each time you exhale you are breathing away your cares, tensions, and fears.

Keep doing this exercise for five minutes or until you feel that you have exhausted its value for you. When you are done, thank the God who is for you and for all people the breath of life.

Unwinding Your Body

When you begin to meditate, you will probably need to relax your body. Tension builds in our muscles and joints, and often we do not even realize it. The following systematic meditation for relaxing can help you unwind and rest before God:

With closed eyes, spend several moments breathing deeply and slowly. Then concentrate on your feet. Feel them inside your shoes or socks against the floor. Consciously tighten or stretch the muscles in your feet and hold them that way for five seconds. Then consciously allow them to relax. Tighten or stretch them again for five seconds, then relax. Now move to your calf muscles and repeat the process. Become conscious of your calf muscles, tighten them, relax, tighten again, and then relax.

Do this process with the different parts of your body in sequence: feet, calves, thighs, stomach and abdomen, shoulders and upper back, hands, arms, chest, neck, head, and face. Or follow a sequence that feels natural to you. The key is to be conscious of tightening and relaxing one part at a time. At each moment a particular part of your body gets the whole focus of your attention. When you are completely relaxed, just rest for a few minutes in the peace of God.

Body Awareness

Close your eyes. Relax. Breathe deeply and slowly, focusing on every breath coming in and going out. Then, beginning with your head and moving down, become conscious of every part of your body. Do not think about your body; rather, try to simply feel it, all parts of it, every sensation you can. Feel the touch of your hair against your forehead or ears or neck. Become aware of the touch of your clothes on your shoulders. Focus for a moment on your back touching against the chair . . . your shirt or blouse touching on your arms . . . your hands touching one another or resting on your lap . . . your buttocks and thighs touching the chair or floor . . . your feet touching within your shoes or against the floor.

Repeat the exercise: head . . . shoulders . . . arms . . . right hand . . . left hand . . . thighs . . . feet. Repeat it again if time allows.

Thank God for the gift of your body. Be mindful all day of its wonderful workings.

(This exercise is based on one by De Mello, in *Sadhana,* pages 15–16.)

Listening with God

Simply pondering the goodness of creation can be a wonderful form of meditation. However, at times, we may wish to sit and "listen" with God, to focus particularly on being in God's presence. Listening meditation can take dozens of forms. Here are a few flexible ways of meditating to be with God. Read the directions carefully and remember them before you actually enter into the meditation. If you forget some steps, do not become anxious. Just be with God. Try each meditation several times, reviewing the directions before each experience.

Resting with God in a Special Place

Most of us have a favorite environment where we find peacefulness: a lakeshore at sunset, a park, the roof of the apartment building under a full moon. Such settings may help us sense the presence of God. Jesus himself prayed on mountaintops and in lonely desert spots. Our imagination can carry us to our favorite places, no matter how ordinary our real environment is. In this exercise you are invited to choose a favorite setting and then imagine yourself there with God.

Before starting to meditate, identify an environment that you like, an actual place you have been that makes you feel peaceful or reflective. Perhaps you have even prayed there before. Then close your eyes and take a few minutes to focus your attention with relaxation exercises and deep breathing.

When you are focused, begin to imagine yourself in the place you have chosen. Use as many of your senses as you can to make the place real to you. Try to see all the details of the place with your mind's eye; smell the aromas that fill the air; hear all the sounds, including those that might not immediately be identified; feel the air touching your skin. Totally immerse yourself in the place.

When you feel yourself at rest, speak to God from your heart. You may find it helpful to imagine Jesus present, or you may want to speak to God alone or to the Spirit. Do what feels most natural and comfortable to you.

After you have shared your thoughts and feelings with God, try to imagine God's responding to you. This may not be in words; it may simply be God's presence around you as you rest, with everything in your environment "speaking" to you of God.

Palms Down, Palms Up

Palms down, palms up is another simple meditation that can be done anywhere and anytime to put you in touch with God.

Close your eyes. Relax, but keep your back erect. If you need to stretch, do so. Rest your hands on your knees with your palms down. Breathe deeply and slowly, inviting the Spirit of God in with each breath.

Placing your hands with the palms down indicates your desire to turn over any concerns, worries, anxieties, or fears to God, who loves you. Let any apprehensions or angry thoughts come to your mind; allow yourself to feel them. Then hand each one over to God in a prayer such as, "Dear God, I give you my worry about . . ." Whatever is weighing your spirit down, release it, with your palms down, as if you were dropping it into God's hand. Let God take it.

When you have handed over each burden to God, turn your hands palm up as a sign of your desire to receive from God. Ask God for the graces you need right now. Let yourself feel whatever comes.

Rest in God's presence. Listen. Attend to God's Spirit speaking from the depths of your heart. If images or guidance come, well and good; if you find only calm silence, be content.

Centering Prayer

Meditation on a single word can draw us close to God. This prayer form is common to most of the world's great religions. Its Christian formulation can be found in a book called *The Cloud of Unknowing,* by an English priest of the fourteenth century. He explains centering prayer this way:

If you want to gather all your desire into one simple word that the mind can easily retain, choose a short word rather than a long one. A one-syllable word such as "God" or "love" is best. But choose one that is meaningful to you. Then fix it in your mind so that it will remain there come what may. This word will be your defense in conflict and in peace. Use it to beat upon the cloud of darkness above you and to subdue all distractions, consigning them to the *cloud of forgetting* beneath you. (William Johnston, editor, page 56)

A single word can be powerful. When fire breaks out, everyone is galvanized into action by the cry "Fire!" This one word penetrates all barriers to attention.

Centering prayer follows these steps: First, sit relaxed and still yourself by stretching and deep breathing. Acknowledge God's presence with you. Then choose a single, holy word that somehow expresses your feeling about being with God. It can be a name of God or another sacred word, such as *Savior, Love, Jesus, Light,* or *Friend.* Begin repeating this word inwardly. You may find it helpful to repeat the word in harmony with your breathing. If your mind wanders or you get distracted, gently pray your holy word again. When you are finished, pray the Lord's Prayer.

Guided Meditation

Guided meditations are designed to help us focus on a theme. They can involve imaging Jesus, some figure of God, or a significant person as part of the process, but they do not have to. The following meditation is about love. By altering the directions, it could be focused on any theme that you wish to explore in meditation: your relationship with God, your future, a particular fear you are struggling with. Guided meditations tap into the ability to imagine, but with a guide or a script to take you through the process. This form of prayer helps us see and hear ourselves and others in new ways in our own mind.

Guided meditations are often done in groups, such as at a retreat or in a class, with the leader reading the script aloud and everyone following along within themselves. To do a guided meditation by yourself, you will need to have a tape recording of the script available and ready in your place of prayer. You or someone else can record the script in a calm, relaxed, slow voice. In the script that follows, ellipses (. . .) indicate a pause. At these points in recording or reading the script, the reader should allow enough silence for those meditating to imagine the scene suggested. Then the reader moves on to the next part of the instructions.

The script opens with suggestions for centering. Feel free to replace these with other directions if you have found another centering technique that works well for you.

Assume your favorite prayer posture. . . . Relax. . . . Let all tension leave your body. . . . Breathe deeply in and out. . . . Feel the tension leave your feet . . . your legs. . . . Relax your stomach and chest. . . . Let all the tension escape your arms . . . and your neck. . . . Let your jaw and face relax. . . . Slow down. . . . Breathe in and out slowly. . . .

Imagine taking a long walk.

Now imagine taking a long walk. . . . See and feel yourself walking slowly through a clearing in a woods. . . . Tall grass and wildflowers wave in a soft breeze. . . . The sun caresses your face. . . . You stop to take in the scene. . . . Birds flit among the flowers and fly into the pine trees ahead of you. . . . Butterflies float among the flowers. . . . One stops near you. . . . You barely breathe so that it won't fly away. . . . You inhale the fragrances carried on the wind. . . . You breathe in and out deeply several times. . . .

You continue to walk slowly toward the woods. . . . A man sits on a log in the shade. . . . With a slight wave of his hand, he invites you to share the log with him. . . . When you are close, he says, "Peace be with you." . . . Your eyes are opened and you know that he is Jesus. . . . You look deeply into his eyes. . . .

Jesus reaches out and takes your hand in his and says, "I love you with an everlasting love." . . . Softly he says: "Now, my friend, tell me of the people you love. Share with me stories of those you love and who love you." . . . You see before you the faces of several people you love. . . . You tell Jesus about the loved ones who reside deeply in your heart. . . . He listens carefully. . . . [Allow a longer pause here.]

When you are finished, Jesus stands to go, saying, "Your sins are forgiven because you have loved much." He embraces you.

. . . Then you watch as he walks slowly into the forest. . . . When he has disappeared, you gaze at the scene around you once more. . . .

When you are ready, return from the scene and open your eyes.

When you finish doing a guided meditation, spend some time writing your reflections and reactions.

The Beginning and the End of Christian Meditation

Some meditation techniques, such as relaxation, centering, body awareness, and breathing awareness, are remarkably similar to methods used to boost personal performance. People who want to improve in athletics, academics, sales, public speaking, or any area where the mind-body relationship and stress reduction are important have come upon meditation as a useful and powerful tool.

However, the beginning and the end of Christian meditation, its source and its goal, are union with God in Jesus Christ. Christian meditation can use many of the techniques developed to quiet and calm the mind and body, but it does not exist for that purpose alone, nor to enhance a person's performance. Rather, the calmness and clearness that come with practicing basic meditation techniques are to allow us to meet God more freely in the silence of our heart. Being alive to God dwelling within us, we become capable of truly loving and serving others with God's own heart.

8

Praying with the Scriptures

Nourished by the Word

If we want to grow in the Christian life—which is what prayer is all about—we need to be fed and nurtured. The Eucharist offers us essential sustenance. Another kind of "food and drink" that enriches the spiritual life of Christians is the record of our faith tradition itself, the Bible.

The Word of God: A Banquet for the Spirit

The Bible is a sacred book in two parts: the Hebrew Scriptures (also known as the Old Testament) and the Christian Testament (also called the New Testament). The whole Bible comprises many smaller "books," some lengthy and some quite brief. In the Catholic version of the Bible, the Hebrew Scriptures consist of forty-six books, and the Christian Testament contains twenty-seven books, for a total of seventy-three books. The Hebrew Scriptures tell the story of God's sacred Covenant with the people of Israel. The Christian Testament shows the fulfillment of that Covenant in Jesus.

The Scriptures offer the spirit a feast as rich and varied as the finest banquet. The "menu" is composed of many types of writing: stories, legends and myths, histories, oracles, conversations, letters, novels, lists, biographies, laws, speeches, poems, parables, proverbs and bits of advice, wise teachings, songs, and prayers. Written at various times and places for many different purposes and audiences, the Scriptures reflect the experience of a people who knew that God was alive and working in their midst.

Inspired by God

For Christians the Scriptures are the word of God. They are the expression of God's love and truth in the experience of God's people; thus they are inspired by God. *Inspired* does not mean that God dictated the words of the Scriptures to their human writers or literally put the words in the mind of those writers. In fact, much of the Scriptures began not in written form but as oral traditions, passed on by word of mouth from generation to generation. God's inspiration happened throughout that whole process, not simply at the moment that pen was put to parchment. Christians believe that God was forming the whole people by way of their experiences; thus God's truth and wisdom were communicated through the writers of the Scriptures.

The writers' choice of literary styles and words, and their cultural traditions, varying purposes, and methods of reaching their audience all contributed to the shape that God's truth and wisdom took in the actual Scriptures. Then the early church leaders decided which writings of the ancient Jews and the early Christians were considered truly authoritative, that is, inspired by God. The list of the seventy-three books they selected is called the Canon. So the writers and the selectors worked with God to convey God's love, mercy, justice, and infinite wisdom in what they wrote down and in what they chose.

Truth, Not Fact

We cannot expect of the ancient storytellers and writers a scientific understanding of the world or historical accuracy in all details. The Scriptures contain inconsistencies and exaggerations, but these simply reflect the human limits and purposes of the writers. They do not take away from the reality that the Scriptures are the inspired word of God. The purpose of the Bible, after all, is to convey religious truth, not scientific or historical fact. Novelist Madeleine L'Engle describes it this way:

> The Bible is true. It's not entirely factual, but it's true. That's hard for a lot of people to understand. Fact and truth are not the same. I love what Karl Barth [a theologian] said: "I take the Bible far too seriously to take it literally."
>
> Some of the Bible is history and some of the Bible is story, and we don't always know which is which. But it doesn't matter. What I'm looking for in the Bible is truth. (Dolly K. Patterson, editor, *Questions of Faith,* pages 63–64)

What we find in the Scriptures is not only stories but the Story of our own people as beloved by God. Taken as a whole, all the different literary forms and purposes of the books add up to a nourishing banquet: God's love given to us through our own Story. Though the Bible was written long ago, as the word of God it is forever fresh and relevant to us today.

Some Advice on Approaching the Bible

When you approach the Scriptures with the intention to pray, keep a few pieces of advice in mind:

1. Do not presume that every word of the Bible is literally true. For instance, the account in the Book of Genesis of how Creation came about and how our first parents were formed is not a scientific one. We need to search for the deeper truth behind the Bible's stories—in this instance, that everything in the universe comes from God and that human beings were made from God's love—rather than looking for biology, astronomy, or geography lessons.

2. View particular passages from the Bible in the context of the whole Bible. Ask yourself, What is the overall message of the Scriptures about this? On some issues, different opinions show up in the Bible. For instance, some of the psalms plead with God to crush the enemies of the Israelites or portray God as vengeful. Jesus told his followers to love their enemies and do good to them; vengefulness was not part of his understanding of his Father, whom he tenderly addressed as *Abba* (Daddy). We have to keep reminding ourselves that the writings of the Bible developed over many centuries. The books reflect the culture and beliefs of the periods in which they were written.

3. Seek out study aids for parts of the Bible that seem to need explanation. A Bible study course will help a great deal, if you are fortunate to have one in your local congregation. Also, most libraries have "study Bibles" and biblical commentaries, which give scholarly background on every book and on specific passages of the Bible. These can aid tremendously in figuring out what a puzzling story or passage is all about. Some biblical stories need explanation, or their rich meaning will be lost to us.

◆ Some Christians read the Bible literally, believing that everything in it must be taken as true in the exact way it is written. Have you ever held this view or encountered it in others? What problems might this approach pose for readers of the Bible?

◆ Find a passage or story in the Bible that seems puzzling or is contradicted by some other passage. Look up a commentary on that passage to deepen your insight.

Come to the Feast: Prayerful Reading

Because the Bible is the word of God, the very act of respectfully reading it becomes prayer. If the reader pays close attention and stays open to what the Holy Spirit says in the Scriptures, prayer takes place. After all, prayer is a kind of conversation with God. Careful reading is a way of listening to God speaking to us.

The Christian community has traditionally urged people to pray by reading the Bible. This form of prayer is called *lectio divina,* meaning "holy reading." Christians have been praying the Bible by simply reading it for nearly two thousand years.

A Process for Prayerful Reading

People develop their own way of reading the Scriptures prayerfully, but one effective way is outlined here just to help you start. This method may be used by an individual or, with modification, by a group. It is an extension of the meditation prayer.

1. First select a scriptural passage to read. Then let yourself quiet down, relax, and remember that God dwells with you. Allow several minutes for this.
2. Read the scriptural passage slowly to yourself. If you are in a group, one person can read aloud for the others.
3. Focus on one line or phrase that catches your attention. Repeat the line or phrase slowly several times to yourself, letting its meaning become more clear to you. If you are in a group, persons can be invited to share aloud the line or phrase they have focused on.
4. Read your passage again slowly and carefully.
5. Let arise from your heart a prayer response based on the line or phrase you found significant. If you are in a group, persons can offer their prayers aloud, with a few moments of silence after each prayer.
6. Again, slowly read your passage.

7. Reflect on this question: How does this passage touch my life at this particular time? If you are in a group, individuals might share their reflections.
8. Close the time of prayerful reading with the Lord's Prayer.

A Sample of Prayerful Reading

Suppose a person named Joel has decided to follow the steps to prayerfully read the Scriptures. After Joel has put himself in a quiet frame of mind, relaxed, and reflected on God's presence with him, he reads this story from the Gospel of Luke:

> Now [Jesus] was teaching in one of the synagogues on the sabbath. And just then there appeared a woman with a spirit that had crippled her for eighteen years. She was bent over and was quite unable to stand up straight. When Jesus saw her, he called her over and said, "Woman, you are set free from your ailment." When he laid his hands on her, immediately she stood up straight and began praising God. But the leader of the synagogue, indignant because Jesus had cured on the sabbath, kept saying to the crowd, "There are six days on which work ought to be done; come on those days and be cured, and not on the sabbath day." But the Lord answered him and said, "You hypocrites! Does not each of you on the sabbath untie his ox or his donkey from the manger, and lead it away to give it water? And ought not this woman, a daughter of Abraham whom Satan bound for eighteen long years, be set free from this bondage on the sabbath day?" When he said this, all his opponents were put to shame; and the entire crowd was rejoicing at all the wonderful things that he was doing. (13:10–17)

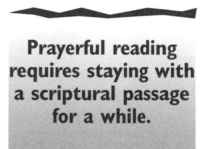

Prayerful reading requires staying with a scriptural passage for a while.

As he finishes the passage, the words "ought not this woman . . . be set free?" stick in Joel's mind. Although unsure why they are significant to him, Joel stays with them and turns them over in his mind, repeating them to himself several times.

As Joel reads the whole passage again, he realizes that he has been feeling terribly unfree lately, tied in knots by a lot of things. He is really longing for freedom—freedom from his hot temper, freedom from his dislike of his sister-in-law, freedom from his fear of failure in his research profession. He turns this captivity over to God in a prayer:

> God, I need to be free of a lot that has been weighing me down—like getting angry too quickly and getting surly when an experiment yields no results. And I'm tired of carrying on this campaign against my sister-in-law. Holy God, help me live more freely in your grace.

One more time, Joel reads to himself the passage about the bent-over woman. He reflects:

> I don't think of myself as an old woman bent over and crippled, but in a certain way I can identify with her. Really it's easy to get all twisted up with problems and being angry about things. I think it would be great if Jesus came along and straightened me out. It feels like it could take a miracle sometimes to get free. Probably everyone needs some kind of healing—myself included. Thank you, Jesus, for being with me, for extending to me your healing grace.

Joel ends his time of prayerful reading and reflection with the Lord's Prayer.

◆ Choose one or more of these scriptural passages and read it prayerfully, following the process outlined on page 116:
  —Genesis 1 (God creates the world.)
  —Exodus 16:4–15 (God sends food to the Israelites.)
  —Psalm 139 (God knows us.)
  —Matthew 20:1–16 (Jesus tells the parable of the laborers in the vineyard.)

—John 8:2–11 (A woman is caught in adultery.)
—Acts 20:7–12 (A young man is restored to life.)
—1 John 4:7–21 (God is love.)
—1 Peter 1:22–23 (Sincerely love other believers.)
—Romans 8:31–39 (Nothing can separate us from God's love.)
—Mark 14:3–9 (The sinful woman anoints Jesus and is forgiven.)
—Luke 6:37–42 (Do not judge other people.)

Pouring Out Your Soul: The Psalms

The Book of Psalms in the Hebrew Scriptures is a collection of 150 prayers that were originally sung by the ancient Israelites. Many of the psalms are traditionally attributed to Israel's King David as writer and composer, but we know from scriptural scholarship that probably numerous psalmists created these sung prayers over several centuries.

Today the psalms are the everyday prayers of Jews, and Christians too pray or sing them in their daily liturgical worship. Over the centuries, composers have put the psalms to the musical styles of their own period. If you examine a hymnal in your church, you will likely find that many of its songs are based on psalms.

Expressing Every Emotion

In ancient Israel the psalms brought together the deepest emotions and religious beliefs of the Jewish people. Reading the psalms or hearing them sung is like listening in on the intense, honest, emotional conversation of lovers who are not afraid to be themselves with each other, even when being themselves does not present a pretty picture. The psalms were not limited to expressing positive sentiments. The ancient Jews poured out praise, thanks, wonder, and joy, but also struggle, guilt, doubt, fear, anger, and even hatred. In their psalms they shared everything about their life and experience with God.

Often when we talk to other people, we tend to cover up what we really feel and think. We shape our talk to fit the audience. The Psalmists, in their talking with God, did not cover up anything. So some psalms sound dangerous, brutal, and mean-spirited because the Psalmist felt that way. The Psalmists even called down God's vengeance on their enemies.

Usually when people think of prayer, they do not consider bringing such negative feelings and harsh wishes to God. But the Psalmists knew they could not fool God. Even if they wanted to make a good impression, they realized that God knew all along what was in their heart and on their mind: sometimes vengeance, hatred, and violence, at other times thanksgiving, wonder, and love.

By praying the psalms, people offer everything in their heart to God. Praying the psalms helps them be honest with God and with themselves. When people pray a psalm of lament, such as Psalm 22, they pour out their anxiety and misery. And they often may find release from their fear by turning their worries over to God's care.

> My God, my God, why have you forsaken me?
> Why are you so far from helping me, from the
>   words of my groaning?
> O my God, I cry by day, but you do not answer;
>   and by night, but find no rest.
>
> .   .   .   .
>
> All who see me mock at me;
>   they make mouths at me, they shake their heads.
>
> (Psalm 22:1–7)

Other psalms give voice to people's thanksgiving for God's many gifts. For instance, Psalm 139 offers thanks and praise to God for the gift of being created:

> For it was you who formed my inward parts;
>   you knit me together in my mother's womb.
> I praise you, for I am fearfully and wonderfully made.
>   Wonderful are your works;
> that I know very well.
>
> (Verses 13–14)

In short, the psalms lend us words to express our sorrows and joys, worries and thanks to the God who listens and cares. In giving voice to these strong feelings, people often find consolation and some freedom from fear and from the need to do acts of vengeance. Instead of letting anger boil over into deeds of violence, they pray the psalms to help them let go of the hatred and help them let God oversee events.

Making a Psalm Our Own

Although the psalms were written ages ago, they express sentiments that are timeless and universal to human experience. They are not simply "someone else's thing" or "some other culture's thing." The psalms can connect intimately with the life of each person who prays them today. However, to make the prayers of the psalms our own, we sometimes have to do a bit of "translation."

Translating to Our Own Experience

Consider, for example, this excerpt from Psalm 56:

All day long foes oppress me;
my enemies trample on me all day long,
for many fight against me.

(Verses 1–2)

Most of us can picture people who dislike us and would do evil against us, and that is certainly what the person who composed Psalm 56 had in mind. Many of the psalms refer to such persecution. But for one of these psalms to be true for us, we do not have to focus on actual persons as enemies. Our adversaries may be oppression from unjust laws; fear of being beaten, robbed, or raped; envy toward other people; hatred for our body; or self-pity. Thus, when we pray this line from verse 7 of Psalm 56, "in wrath cast down the peoples, O God!" we can mean it, but we are translating the peoples the Psalmist had in mind to other "enemies" that are real for us. We want God to bring ruin to those enemies—to injustice, self-hatred, and other evils we might be suffering—not necessarily to actual persons. We can let our own anger and desire for vengeance be purged as we express ourselves using the Psalmist's words.

Likewise, psalms of joy and gratitude for specific things can be translated into prayers that express what we ourselves are grateful for. If a psalm praises God for the sea and the sky, but you never experience the sea because you live in a desert, you can still be grateful for the natural world around you that you do experience. *Sea* and *sky* can be thought of as symbols for all varieties of creation.

◆ Write your own psalm of thanksgiving, including many different things you are grateful for. Begin your psalm with the opening words of Psalm 138, "I give you thanks, O LORD, with my whole heart."

Making the Unknown Familiar

Perhaps the most familiar psalm to Christians is Psalm 23, "The LORD is my shepherd" (verse 1). With this prayer, we run into a gap in understanding if we do not know anything about shepherding or sheep. To appreciate the full feeling of the original psalm, we need to get in touch with the experience of the ancients for whom keeping sheep was a familiar part of life.

People of the Eskimo culture, who have no experience of sheep, translated Psalm 23 to speak of what they *do* know keenly—the relationship between a dog and its master. As a symbol of their relationship to God, the trust between a husky team dog and its master was much more fitting than the reliance of a sheep on its shepherd. Here is how they translated the psalm:

> The Lord is my master: I am his dog.
> He makes me lie down in soft snow;
> He leads me across firm ice:
> He calls to me encouragingly.
> He drives me on good trails because I belong to Him.
> Through storms and troubles, I will not be afraid
>   because He is with me,
> My harness is securely fastened
> And his hand is on the sled.
> He guards me while I eat, though enemies lurk near.
> He doctors my hurts.
> My heart overflows with gratitude.

Only kindness and gentle care will be mine from the
    hands of this master
And I will be on his team forever.
        (From C. Renée Rust, *Making the Psalms Your Prayer,*
        page 34)

◆ Make Psalm 23 your own. Rewrite the psalm, replacing the
sheep and shepherd with an image that means something to you.

Appreciating the Jews' Life and History

The lamentation psalms were composed to express the anguish, anger, and grief of the Jewish people while they were in
exile in Babylon. They had been uprooted from their home in
Jerusalem (Zion), where their beloved city and Temple were
destroyed by the Babylonians. They were then brought to the
lush, wealthy city of Babylon, where they were held captive by
the Babylonian king. If we understand what a wrenching experience it was for the Jews to be taken from their home and to
lose forever their dear Temple, we will be better able to make
the lamentation psalms our own. We can identify our own
times of grief, sadness, and longing or homesickness with these
psalms. When we read these lines from Psalm 137, we can pray
from within our own experience:

By the rivers of Babylon—
    there we sat down and there we wept
    when we remembered Zion.
On the willows there
    we hung up our harps.
For there our captors
    asked us for songs,
and our tormentors asked for mirth, saying,
    "Sing us one of the songs of Zion!"

How could we sing the LORD's song
    in a foreign land?
If I forget you, O Jerusalem,
    let my right hand wither!
Let my tongue cling to the roof of my mouth,
    if I do not remember you,
if I do not set Jerusalem above my highest joy.

        (Verses 1–7)

You may be going through a similar experience of being uprooted from a place you love; maybe you moved, changed jobs, or began retirement. The Israelites' sorrow may be close to your own feelings, and you can pray the psalm as a "fellow exile."

You can also make the psalm your own by considering the ways you are "held captive"—maybe by greed or envy or ignorance or weakness. Zion, or Jerusalem, represents home and freedom.

◆ Write your own lamentation psalm, beginning with these words from Psalm 22: "My God, my God, why have you forsaken me?" (verse 1).

Reflecting on Questions

◆ To get into the spirit of praying the psalms, read Psalm 130 and then reflect on these questions:
—What are some areas of your life in which you need God's mercy and forgiveness?
—In what ways have you felt yourself waiting for God's mercy?
—What image of God do you receive from this psalm?
—How do you feel about the God who is portrayed in this psalm?

◆ Then focus on Psalm 8, reflecting on these questions:
—What image of God is portrayed in this psalm?
—What attributes of God in this psalm are different from the ones in Psalm 130?
—Consider the ways you have been created only "a little lower than God" (verse 5). Do you ordinarily think of yourself in this way?
—How do you experience having "dominion over the works" of God's hands (verse 6)?

Using Your Imagination: Stories and Parables

The Bible as a whole is the Story of God's people. But it is also filled with particular stories. The Hebrew Scriptures tell about heroes and villains and events that show God at work among the people. The Gospels are a series of stories about Jesus. Jesus himself used parables, stories of a kind, to teach truths about God and about how people should relate to one another as God's family.

The ancient Jews and the early Christians knew the power of a story. Stories warn us about dangers and invite us to explore. They tickle our fancy and move us to tears. Stories push us back into memories and project us into the future. They take us down wild, hazardous rivers without getting us wet. They hit us with truth without hurting us. And they touch our whole person—intellect, emotions, and sometimes even body (holding our breath and laughing are bodily responses to stories). Great stories seem to hang on for generations. The Bible is full of such stories, all pointing to the overriding message that God loves us and is faithful to us and that God is looking for a faithful and loving response from us.

The stories in the Scriptures beckon us to dive inside them and experience them with our whole person. To do this we need to actively engage our imagination. Here are a couple of ways, among many, to use our imagination with the stories in the Bible.

Putting Yourself in the Scene

A great way to get inside the stories of the Scriptures is to imagine yourself as a character in them. To do this you need to read the selected passage slowly once or twice, trying to imagine the place, the people, and what happens. It helps also to have some understanding of the context of the story. This is where reading a brief commentary about the story or about the main character in the story greatly adds to its meaning for us.

Suppose, for instance, that we are going to focus on the story of Jesus and the tax collector Zacchaeus, in Luke 19:1–10. First we read the passage slowly and carefully. By consulting a biblical commentary on this passage, such as *The Collegeville Bible Commentary,* we piece together a bit more of the context of the story. It is especially helpful to know that Jewish tax collectors were working for the Roman authorities and were thus seen more or less as traitors to their own people. Also, most of them tended to make a handsome sum by taking a proportion of the collections for themselves. They were viewed as cheating the poor. Being marginal to their own people and considered sinners, these men were not

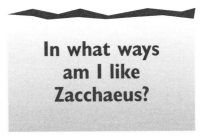

In what ways am I like Zacchaeus?

particularly observant of Jewish practices. So a tax collector's reputation had several strikes against it. Thus, for Jesus to pick out a tax collector from the crowd and invite himself to dinner at the collector's house would have raised quite a few eyebrows among the Jews who were jockeying to receive Jesus' special attention.

With that background in mind, we then reread the story, this time zeroing in on one character with whom we identify. Zacchaeus himself is our choice. Then we enter into a time of meditation, imagining ourselves telling the account from Zacchaeus's point of view.

As with other meditations, we need to wind down in order to really put ourselves into it. So we relax our whole body by breathing deeply and stretching. Sitting with both feet planted on the ground and our hands resting on our legs helps, too. When we are relaxed, we try to put ourselves into the scene as the character we have identified with. We re-enact the scene in our imagination, vividly sensing the sights, smells, sounds, tastes, and feelings.

We find plenty of material to explore prayerfully once we have gotten inside the story from this one character's point of view. We could reflect on questions like these suggested by the story:

- In what ways am I like Zacchaeus?
- If I were Zacchaeus and Jesus had come for a visit at my house, what would our conversation sound like?
- What would it feel like to have someone see the good in me that no one else seems to see?
- If I experienced unqualified love like Jesus had for Zacchaeus, would it make me change anything about my life?

◆ Here are some other Gospel stories about Jesus that could be used like the story of Zacchaeus. Choose one of them and imagine it from the point of view of one of the characters. Reflect afterward with questions suggested by your imaginary retelling.
  Mark 10:17 22 (The rich young man turns away.)
—John 13:1–16 (Jesus washes the Apostles' feet.)
—Luke 17:11–19 (Jesus cures the ten lepers.)
—Luke 2:1–12 (Jesus is born.)
—Mark 15:21–39 (Jesus is crucified.)
—Mark 16:1–8 (Jesus is raised from the dead.)
—John 11:17–44 (Jesus brings Lazarus back to life.)
—Luke 7:36–50 (Jesus forgives the sinful woman.)

Retelling a Parable

The stories that Jesus told to illustrate his message are called parables. These were designed to help people understand something that they would ordinarily not see as applying to themselves. By drawing his listeners in with a fascinating story, Jesus was able to hold their attention because they wanted to learn how the story turned out. Then, often with a surprise ending, Jesus would make a point that was usually a bit uncomfortable for his listeners to hear.

> **Jesus used everyday experiences in his parables, to bring home lessons to his listeners.**

One way to make a parable especially relevant to our own life is to retell it as a contemporary story. As with the other stories in the Bible, it helps to know the background of a parable and to have some idea of the meaning intended by Jesus. Once we have gotten this far, we can translate the story into our own context, giving it fresh meaning.

Let's take, for example, the popular parable of the good Samaritan (Luke 10:25–37). Before we can translate the parable into our own situation, we need to know several things that can be found out from *The Collegeville Bible Commentary,* and from the *Dictionary of the Bible,* by John L. McKenzie, under the entry "Samaritans." For one, Jesus was addressing an audience of Jews who exaggerated the importance of the proper observance of Jewish laws and practices. The Jewish priests and Levites in particular tended to do so. In their mind God's favor was restricted to a select, inside group. A despised, outside group was the Samaritans, who were "distant cousins" of the mainline Jews. Because they had different rituals than did the main body of Judaism, Samaritans were thought to be inferior and unclean. Yet, in this parable, Jesus makes them exemplary in the ability to "love their neighbor."

Jesus' parables were meant to be highly relevant to their audience. He used the everyday experiences of the people as material for them, and that is one reason they were very effective. As a way to bring them home to us and help them speak to our life, recasting parables into our own setting can be a rich source of prayer and reflection.

◆ The following parables lend themselves well to retelling in contemporary terms. Choose one and write or tell aloud your own version.
   —Matthew 18:23–35 (The unforgiving servant)
   —Luke 12:16–21 (The rich fool)
   —Matthew 18:12–14 or Luke 15:4–7 (The lost sheep)
   —Luke 15:11–32 (The prodigal son)
   —Luke 18:9–14 (The Pharisee and the tax collector)

Like a Harvest of Grapes

In prayer, people enter into conversation and relationship with God. We talk; God listens. God talks; we listen. The Bible is a central way in which God "talks" to humankind. If we pray with the Scriptures, we listen to what God is trying to communicate to us about the meaning of life, and our response is attuned to God's ways.

The Scriptures are like a harvest of ripe grapes. To be appreciated, the grapes first must be picked. Some may be eaten right away, fresh and juicy. Some may be set aside, crushed, and fermented to make wine, which is then tasted slowly, rolled on the tongue to capture the full flavor, and swallowed. Consumed fresh or imbibed in fine wine, the grapes provide nourishment and joy. So too with the Scriptures. Some passages can be understood and accepted easily; others take more time, study, and prayer to be appreciated and valued. Ultimately the Scriptures nourish and bring joy because they convey the basic truth that God loves us unconditionally and forever.

9

COMMUNITY PRAYER

BINDING US TOGETHER WITH GOD

We live in community—in our family, in our profession, among friends, with fellow volunteers, perhaps in a parish group. We may experience community in our neighborhood, at work, on a volunteer board, in an orchestra or choir or drama group, even standing in line for hours with hundreds of others to buy tickets to a sports event.

We may feel more or less connected with a given community based on how much we sense we have in common with the others in it, how much the members care about one another and support one another, how much they even know about one another. Community members can be incredibly diverse in talents, skills, and personalities but still feel joined with one another. Something deeper than mere sameness unites them. People are drawn to the deeper connections of community, perhaps because they sense that they will discover and express their true selves in those bonds.

Even an adult group studying prayer can become a strong community, if the participants share with one another who they are—their strengths and weaknesses, joys and sorrows, hopes and fears.

Community Rituals: United Through Words and Actions

One feature that binds people together as a community is ritual. Communal rituals have been an essential part of every culture in all eras of human history. Through words and symbolic actions, rituals celebrate what is meaningful to the group or culture. A ritual can be repeated over and over and yet sustain its power to bind people together because it expresses something important in a community's identity and experience.

Ritual as a Universal Human Need

Human beings naturally gather to celebrate, to mourn, to feast, to acknowledge important events. Some communal rituals have formal structures and set patterns. Others are created as circumstances dictate. Regardless of the form these rituals take, gathering for them with friends, relatives, and neighbors is an age-old human need.

The variety of community rituals is nearly boundless. Here are a few examples—some exotic, some familiar:

After forty years of employment at Standard Fixtures, Mary knows what she can expect at her retirement party. The company's president will say a few words of appreciation. One of her friends will tell stories about her. The boss will present her with a plaque and a gift. Finally, she will say a few words; she will cut the ceremonial cake; and then, after applause, she and her coworkers will eat and visit.

◆

Since anyone can remember, the graduating seniors at Saint Edward's High School have marched in to commencement to the sound of the "Wedding March" from the opera *Aida*. Every year, the salutatorian offers the invocation, the valedictorian delivers a five-minute speech, the diplomas are distributed by the principal, and the graduates give three cheers for their parents. As they march out, the graduates sing the school fight song.

◆

On the Pacific Island of Vanuatu, adolescent boys dive off a fifty-foot tower with elastic vines strapped to their ankles—vines that will jerk them to a halt just before they smash into the ground. By leaping off the tower, the boys prove their manhood to the community, and they are then honored by extravagant feasting.

◆

In Bali, Indonesia, young men and women who want to marry must have their upper front teeth filed down in a ritual before the whole community. An ancient Hindu belief holds that this symbolic act will reduce the force of human passions.

◆

Many American Indian communities ritualize the changes in seasons. In spring they celebrate corn planting with dances and songs. To bring needed rain, one tribe sings:
   White floating clouds,
   Clouds like eagle down,
   Come and water the earth.

◆

Fans of the Olympic Games gather to watch the opening ceremony. After the parade of the teams and a glittering show, a lone runner appears carrying the Olympic torch. The games officially begin only when the torch ignites a huge flame.

Perhaps you were surprised to see a graduation ceremony, a retirement party, or the opening of the Olympics listed as a ritual. These are not particularly religious events, and you may have associated the word *ritual* with religion. But rituals exist in all areas of life; even the process of introducing people and shaking hands is a ritual.

◆ Think of five rituals that you participate in either at home, at church, or in the larger culture.
◆ Ponder how one of these rituals contributes to your life and to the life of the community.

Communal Prayer as "Building Up"

A ritual that is intended to bring people together to an awareness of God and of sacred mystery is a communal prayer. Why
is communal prayer significant to the life of communities? Here
is what Saint Paul told the Christians of Corinth about praying
together: "When you come together, each one has a hymn, a
lesson, a revelation . . . or an interpretation. Let all things be
done for building up" (1 Corinthians 14:26).

Paul knew that the fledgling communities of Christians
needed to be nurtured and built up. People pray together because they can strengthen one another and their community as
a whole. Communal prayer creates bonds in a way that no other activity can. As Paul suggested, during prayer people can
share their insights, gifts, stories, and lessons with one another.
But more than that, because they do this consciously *with God,*
they receive strength from a source beyond themselves. When
people are aware of their relationship with God and one another, communal prayer can unite and affirm them in a powerful way.

A community that shares its faith and celebrates together
through song and prayer supports the faith of all its members.
In our society it is easy to be discouraged about trying to live
according to Christian faith and values. TV personalities joke
about religion. Stories of violence cover the front page of
newspapers. Song lyrics and advertisements devalue women
and men, showing them as dumb and helpless, as sex objects,
or as cold dominators. A Christian community at prayer stands
opposed to these aspects of contemporary culture. Communal
prayer publicly says: "We seek God and love. We believe in
the dignity and goodness of all that God has made." In communal prayer we deepen our commitment to these values by
reminding one another of what is important to us, what gives
life meaning. As a result our faith can be strengthened.

Praying together also gives us the chance to celebrate with
others. Few things seem more lonely than eating Thanksgiving
dinner solo or sitting at home alone on Christmas. We can celebrate and give thanks alone, but our rejoicing takes on added
energy when we join with others. When we celebrate in community, we have only to look around to realize how God has

blessed us. Other people are God's image; their kindness, help, and friendship are God's kindness, help, and friendship. Communal prayer provides an opportunity to unite in giving thanks.

Jesus told his followers: "'If two of you agree on earth about anything you ask, it will be done for you by my Father in heaven. For where two or three are gathered in my name, I am there among them'" (Matthew 18:19–20). All prayer in Jesus' name has power, but community prayer has special energy. The Christian life is not a solo operation; it is fundamentally communal.

◆ Reflect on your experience of community prayer. What characterizes meaningful community prayer?

Occasions for Communal Prayer

Traditionally people gather in prayer to petition God for help, to give praise and thanks, to seek reconciliation, and sometimes to mark a special occasion. Prayer services contain some or all of these elements.

Asking God's Help

Jesus told his followers to pray for what they needed, especially in twos and threes, meaning in community. During a time of drought, many congregations pray for rain. When someone dies, family and friends join in praying for the deceased person and for relief of their own grief. In time of war, services are held to ask God to protect loved ones and end the violence. If neighbors are sick, people may gather to pray for their healing.

Praising and Thanking God

In times of joy, people give praise and thanks to God. National holidays are often occasions for communities to thank God for freedom gained and gifts given. People of the United States celebrate Thanksgiving, commemorating God's goodness to the English settlers who managed to survive the first year of colonization in New England. Almost every culture celebrates the Creator's kindness for sending rich harvests. Just as people have parties to rejoice, so believers join to praise and thank the source of all goodness.

Reconciling

No group of people is perfect. Inevitably, conflicts break out. School boards have split into factions over the use of financial resources for buildings or for raising teachers' salaries. Fights occur in parishes over liturgical matters or the need to remodel the church. Bitter feelings rend groups over a great variety of issues. One way of healing such rifts is through reconciling prayer, that is, prayer intended to draw people to mutual forgiveness and the beginnings of harmony.

Celebrating Special Occasions

Communities frequently celebrate important occasions with prayer together. Wedding anniversaries, graduations, birthdays, the winning of a championship game—all community events—invite celebration by community prayer. Many prayer services for special occasions combine petition, praise, thanksgiving, and reconciling prayers.

◆ Think back on the last year's events. What might have been good opportunities for communal prayer for your local community, parish, family, and friends?

Creating Community Prayers and Rituals

The Catholic Tradition is known for its beautiful and moving rituals, and in fact for its sense of the power of communal prayer. The official public prayer of the Catholic church is called its liturgy. The liturgy comprises the sacraments of the church (including the Eucharist) as well as the Divine Office (a collection of prayers and scriptural readings). As official public acts of the church, these liturgical rituals have certain fixed features, although they can be modified and do allow for different options in adapting and planning them.

Another kind of communal prayer, one that is not part of the official liturgy, is a simple prayer service. This kind of prayer can be planned from scratch by a person or a group, using some simple guidelines and lots of creativity and spirit. The following guidelines and thoughts from others' experiences can help you create a prayer service.

1. Choose a Topic and a Theme

Many novels and speeches focus on a single idea or thread that runs throughout the whole work. This thread, or theme, unifies all the elements. A theme is more than a topic, which is the general subject of the work; it is the slant your community wants to take on a topic.

For instance, the topic for a prayer service might be peace, and the theme or direction, "Through friendship we are able to understand what true peace is." Or if a student dies in an automobile accident, the topic of a prayer service would be her or his death, and the theme would focus on how the larger community wants to deal with that death and the message it wants to give to that young person's friends, such as, "Do not lose hope; Jesus promised resurrection."

Life constantly points toward subjects to pray about. If some natural catastrophe like a tornado or a flood has occurred, a group may want to pray together about that. If people have become tired of the back stabbing that sometimes haunts the halls of an agency or education center, a prayer about honesty or respecting human dignity might be helpful. Any human experience that confronts us is a fit subject for communal prayer.

The liturgical seasons—Pentecost, Advent, Christmas, Lent, and Easter, for instance—are often occasions for prayer services. During Advent, topics and themes such as these would be appropriate:

Topic	Theme
Waiting	What does it mean to wait for the Messiah?
Promise	We can trust God's promise to save us.
Light	Jesus comes to bring light to our world.
Prepare	Prepare your heart for the coming of Jesus.

During Lent, other topics and themes come to mind:

Topic	Theme
Mercy	How can we show mercy to other people?
Conversion	What is preventing you from turning to God?

The holidays and the seasons of nature can also be a focus of community prayer. A New Year's prayer service might have as its theme "What kind of world do we look forward to in the year ahead?" A Thanksgiving service might focus on the theme "My heart is grateful for all God's gifts to me." On Valentine's Day we might pray on the theme of the many ways God loves us and how we can love God in return. Springtime invites us to offer prayers of thanks and praise for the new life that is coming forth from the earth and maybe in the hearts of our family as well.

◆ What five possible topics for prayer services has life placed before you? These can be from events in your family, from world or national news, or from happenings in your community. To spur your thinking, ask yourself, Is something important going on in my family? Has a particular topic come up continually among my friends? Has a recent event from the news caused a lot of talk? Is something in this community on everyone's mind? Pick one topic and write a theme statement for a prayer service.

◆ What are three holiday or seasonal topics that a community you belong to might celebrate together through prayer? Pick one topic and write a theme statement for a prayer service. You will be asked to develop this prayer service in the activities for steps 2 to 7.

2. Create the Right Environment

The right environment helps a community pray well. Although prayer can take place anywhere, it is aided by a prayerful setting. A chapel or prayer room can be a good spot, but you may have to improvise and design a space within your home.

In creating your prayer service, consider the following questions about the environment:

Is the space the right size? If the room is large, you might arrange the seating in a circle so that people can look at one another rather than out at empty space. If the room is rather small, consider having the participants in a semicircle facing a window or a still-life arrangement, to give a more open feeling. You may want to arrange various types of seating to match different preferences and health needs.

What objects or artifacts will set the right tone? Candles are almost always useful to set a mood as well as to provide some natural light. If you are having a harvest prayer, pumpkins, colorful squash, Indian corn, and scarlet leaves might be arranged in the center of the group of participants. Strings of lights would be fitting for a pre-Christmas prayer service. Choose objects or decorations appropriate to the theme and useful for settling the participants into the mood of your prayer service. You might even put up a poster with your theme written on it.

What sounds will enhance the service? Playing reflective music as participants enter the prayer place can set the right mood. If you are going to use a guided meditation, make sure you have some soothing background music. Also make sure everyone can hear the readings and the music. If you will be in a large place, like a church sanctuary, check microphones and speaker systems, and set music recordings at the right volume.

How can various participants help create the environment? When a prayer service involves the participants, it not only treats a theme but also celebrates and creates community. So some people might make a poster or gather the visual images for the prayer. Others might arrange the space, and others get the music together. When people have a role to play in the planning, they will feel more involved in the prayer itself.

In addition, the people leading the prayer service set the tone and affect the environment by their attitude toward what they are doing. When they are prepared and calm, willing to share themselves and their prayers seriously with the participants, a profound tranquillity and prayerful atmosphere can result. When the leaders then ask the participants to become quiet and enter into prayer together, the participants will be more disposed to get into the spirit of prayer.

Create the proper environment for the holiday or seasonal topic and theme you chose for your prayer service (see the second reflection activity listed on page 135):

◆ What space will you use? How will you arrange the seating to fit the space and to fit your topic and theme?

◆ Considering the theme of your prayer service, how can you set the right tone in the space you will use? What sort of objects or artifacts will you use to establish the best atmosphere?

◆ List some background music that will help to create a prayerful mood as people enter.

◆ Think of a variety of ways that people in your planning group can participate in creating the right environment.

3. Select Readings

One or two readings from the Scriptures or another source may be selected. These readings should provide the participants with some perspective on the theme. For instance, if the prayer theme is "God is with us in all circumstances of our life," a helpful reading might be Romans 8:38–39, in which Paul says, "I am convinced that neither death, nor life, nor angels, nor rulers, nor things present, nor things to come, nor powers, nor height, nor depth, nor anything else in all creation, will be able to separate us from the love of God in Christ Jesus."

To find Bible passages related to a certain theme or topic, refer to a biblical commentary, a dictionary of the Bible, or a concordance. If the topic is Advent or another liturgical season, a reading from a Sunday eucharistic celebration for that season (found in any Sunday missal) might be ideal.

Poems, stories, song lyrics, or paragraphs from magazine articles may also serve as readings for prayer services, and in fact can work well with a scriptural reading. The key consideration in selecting them is that they connect with the theme and can inform or inspire those attending the service. You may even want to use a guided meditation along the lines of the one suggested in chapter 7 (see pages 108–109).

Do not overload a prayer service with too many readings or with selections that are too long. One or two short readings serve best.

All readings should be practiced beforehand. Readers need to make sure they can pronounce words correctly.

Just before a reading, the reader should pause a moment to allow everyone to turn their attention to listening. The title of a poem or story might be given, as well as the reason for selecting the reading with its particular theme. The reader should speak slowly, expressively, and clearly. After the reading the participants should be given a few moments of silence to think about what was said.

◆ Considering the theme of your prayer service, find two readings—at least one of which is from the Bible—that will be helpful and meaningful for participants.

4. Involve People Through Symbolic Action

Effective prayer services often include symbolic actions; these are especially helpful for involving the participants and building a sense of community. A planning group should choose a symbolic action that will not need a lot of explanation, but will relate easily to the theme of the prayer. This often entails some item that is visual or tangible, or some act or movement that gets people to do more than just sit and listen. For instance:

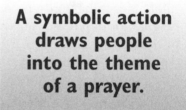

A symbolic action draws people into the theme of a prayer.

• During a prayer about Jesus the Living Water, participants may each be given a glass of cold water. After a reading from John 4:5–30, about Jesus the Living Water, everyone might drink together. (This exercise is especially effective on a hot day.)

• Leaders of a prayer service on peace may give out papers on which the traditional peace symbol is drawn, asking participants to write within the symbol what they could do to bring peace to their own small corner of the world. The participants might then bring these papers forward and tape them onto a large wall poster with Peace Plans written on it.

- Using the theme "Jesus gave himself for us; let us give ourselves for others," leaders may distribute small paper crosses and ask participants to write on the crosses one way that they could give themselves up for someone else. These crosses might be taped to a wall poster in the shape of a cross.

Oil, bread, silver coins, grapevines, pine cones, or some object from everyday life might be used, depending on the theme of a prayer service. Use your imagination in figuring out how to use the symbol, and during the service, approach the action reverently. If a group responds openly and respectfully to ritual action and symbol, the prayer experience can be significant and memorable.

◆ Based on your prayer service theme, devise a symbolic action that is simple but will involve everyone in the community and add meaning to the prayer.
◆ Pick a symbol that can be displayed during your prayer service.

5. Select and Plan for Music

Like almost nothing else, music moves us. Many good songs have insightful lyrics, but even more than that, the tune and rhythm get into our bones. Because effective prayer comes from us as a whole person—body, feelings, and mind—prayer services include music to touch and express our feelings.

Prayer services are commonly opened with a song. Another piece of music may end the service or be used elsewhere. Music may be played for reflective listening, as a starter for a discussion or shared prayer, for people to sing or hum along with—or all of these.

One way of involving people is to ask musicians within the prayer group to play instruments. For instance, a soft and slow acoustic guitar piece may be played at the start of the prayer or during a time of reflection. You may even use soft instrumental music as background for a reading.

You may also use recorded music—cassette tapes, CDs, or videotapes. If you do, the equipment must be preset to the right song and volume. You may want to begin and end a musical selection on a very low volume for a smooth transition.

The music may be popular, classical, or specifically religious, like hymns. Whatever its form, it should relate closely to the theme. The following questions can help in its selection:

- Does the music create the right mood for the theme?
- Is the tempo right for the tone of the prayer service?
- Are the words appropriate to and meaningful for the group?
- If the song will be sung by everyone, is the melody easy to learn, and is the range possible to sing? Are people familiar with the song? (If necessary, ask them.) Are copies of the song readily available? Do you need to practice it first?

Finding just the right music requires effort, but it can add significantly to the power of your prayer together.

◆ Find one hymn to use in your prayer service.
◆ Pick one piece of popular or classical music that will add to the mood and meaning of your prayer.

6. Create a Way to Share Reflections

If members of a group know one another well and respect one another, including a period of shared reflection can make the prayer more personal and more of a community builder. Shared prayer or shared reflection, in which spontaneous prayers or comments are offered aloud, invites people to relate their personal insights to the theme. As a result, participants experience the values, concerns, hopes, and struggles of other people. Participants may feel less alone. Some risk is involved, though. Perhaps only a few people will respond. Someone may offer an offbeat remark. However, most people appreciate the opportunity to share their prayers and reflections.

Shared prayer works best when people are comfortable with one another. If a group has not tried this sort of prayer, start by inviting each member in turn to offer a petition aloud after a reading. Or ask the members to write an anonymous petition on a piece of paper that will be put into a bowl or

bag; then each member of the group in turn can read someone else's petition drawn from the bowl or bag.

When a group has the right level of trust, you may invite
participants to share their personal insights, stories, or reflections about a reading or theme. One technique that helps people start sharing on this level is to allow them to write their
reflections during a period of silence. So, for instance, after a
reading of the parable of the good Samaritan, you might invite
the participants first to write and then to share aloud any ideas
they have about the parable. In this sort of shared prayer, no
one should feel forced to say anything. If you include this type
of shared prayer in a service, be prepared to offer some reflections just to set an example.

It usually helps to focus the sharing by asking for reflections on a specific question. For instance:

- For a service with the theme "Christ, the light of the
  world," you might ask participants to think about someone
  who is a light in their life. Then pass a lighted candle
  around the circle. Each participant may offer a reflection
  when the candle comes to him or her. In this service, participants might talk about an influential companion whom
  they see regularly, or a relative who always listens to and
  encourages them, and so on.

- On the topic of conversion, you might ask participants to
  think of some change they would like to see in the world,
  in their family, or in themselves that would make the future
  better.

- Focusing on "God's promise to us," participants might share
  a promise they made that they are glad they kept.

If limited time is available for a prayer service, shared reflection should probably be omitted. If participants start sharing and time runs out, cutting them off becomes difficult and
may leave people with hurt feelings.

◆ Compose a method of inviting participants to share their reflections, petitions, or prayers of thanks on the theme of your
prayer service.

7. Put It All Together

A prayer service needs to be structured to fit the group, the theme, the time allotted, and the elements chosen. Here is one way a prayer service may be structured:

1. Welcome, call to remember God's presence, and invitation to the theme
2. Opening song
3. Common prayer (an original prayer, a psalm, and so on)
4. First reading
5. Pause for silent reflection
6. Second reading (one reading should be scriptural)
7. Shared prayer or petitions, symbolic action, silent time accompanied by music, or some combination of these
8. Closing prayer
9. Final song

◆ Structure a prayer service, using the elements discussed in this chapter. If you have a group with whom you pray, prepare any needed handouts and materials. Ask for help from other group participants. In short, be ready to lead the prayer service for the whole group.

8. Evaluate the Experience

Those who compose and lead prayer services can profit from feedback from the group afterward. Being able to assess the effectiveness of a service may help everyone to create better prayer experiences in the future.

You might want to ask participants about their comfort level during the prayer, their feelings of involvement, what they liked best, and what was hardest for them. It will be helpful for you and the other prayer leaders to think back and talk about how prepared you were, how the pace went, whether and how you created the right tone and atmosphere, and so on.

God at Work in Our Community

Praying with other people is an adventure. Even a well-planned prayer service turns up surprises, and that is probably a welcome sign that God, not just our own efforts and plans, is at work. What people get out of the readings may be completely different from what the leaders have imagined. A shared prayer may uncap rich reservoirs of experience or end in comfortable silence. After all, the Holy Spirit moves in various and amazing ways.

Praying together has a power and dynamic different from that of praying privately. Communal prayer teaches us lessons we cannot learn alone. It is an opportunity for mutual support in faith, hope, and love, a time to celebrate together who we are and *whose* we are.

10

THE EUCHARIST

CELEBRATING JESUS' SAVING PRESENCE

The Eucharist, or Mass, has always been a central ritual of the church's liturgy. An early eucharistic experience can throw fresh light on our understanding of the Eucharist today. In the story as told in Luke's Gospel, two of Jesus' followers were walking along the road from Jerusalem to Emmaus, sad and discouraged by Jesus' horrible Crucifixion and baffled by the reports of his Resurrection. A stranger, who was really Jesus, joined them and asked what they were talking about.

The two disciples did not recognize Jesus in the stranger. Amazed that this person had not heard the news, they hurried to tell him about Jesus the prophet, "mighty in deed and word before God and all the people" (Luke 24:19). They told the stranger about Jesus' Crucifixion, about their dashed hopes that he would save Israel from oppression, and about reports of his Resurrection. In reply, by referring to the Hebrew Scriptures, the stranger showed them that the one they were mourning indeed was the Messiah. Still the disciples did not recognize him as Jesus. Night began to fall as they reached Emmaus. The disciples, fascinated by this "stranger," urged him to stay on with them. The story concludes this way:

> When [Jesus] was at the table with [the disciples], he took bread, blessed and broke it, and gave it to them. Then their eyes were opened, and they recognized him; and he vanished from their sight. They said to each other, "Were not our hearts burning within us while he was talking to us on the road, while he was opening the scriptures to us?" That same hour they got up and returned to Jerusalem; and they found the eleven and their companions gathered together. They were saying, "The Lord has risen indeed, and he has appeared to Simon!" Then they told what had happened on the road, and how he had been made known to them in the breaking of the bread. (Luke 24:30–35)

In the blessing, breaking, and sharing of bread, the disciples of Jesus recognized him. In a revealing moment, the meaning of what had happened in the past became clear to them. The suffering, discouragement, and seeming failure they had been experiencing were transformed into joy by the recognition that Jesus was truly risen and with them.

At the Eucharist today, Jesus still speaks to us as the Scriptures are opened to us. He still breaks the bread of his own life with us. And with faith and hope, believers' hearts today can burn within them. Like the disciples on the road to Emmaus, we are travelers on life's road. We can find the meaning of our life experiences in the breaking and sharing of bread with Jesus and one another.

Celebrating the Greatest Gift

The Last Supper, held the night before Jesus died, was the occasion for the first Eucharist. The Emmaus story tells of another Eucharist a few days later. This ritual became central for the early Christians as they sought to remember the Risen Jesus after his Ascension. Through the Eucharist, the community celebrates God's greatest gift to humanity: Jesus Christ. People are also called to bring their own life to the table of Jesus, uniting themselves with the paschal mystery—Jesus' life, death, and Resurrection.

A Reflection of What We Bring

In a well-celebrated Eucharist, people consciously bring their own joys and sorrows, triumphs and failures, dreams and fears to the table. In this way they unite themselves with Jesus and enter into the saving power of the paschal mystery. However, because the participants are human, they are limited, and thus the ritual is not always celebrated well. Those coming to Mass may be truly present and involved, or they may be simply going through the motions.

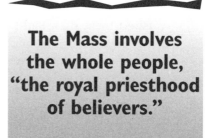

The Mass involves the whole people, "the royal priesthood of believers."

They may sing from the heart and soul, or only halfheartedly. The readings may be proclaimed in a way that strikes to the core, or they may be poorly delivered and hard to understand.

Precisely because the Eucharist is celebrated by humans, we might be tempted not to take the ritual seriously. Few Masses have the dazzle of a professional football game, the allure of an award-winning film, or the energy of Handel's *Messiah* performed at Christmastime. Next to these, the Mass could seem tame and maybe drab.

But the Mass is not a performance to be watched; it makes demands on us to participate. For the Eucharist to have meaning for people, they have to be significantly involved in it. Referring to "the royal priesthood of believers," the official instructions for the Mass say that "the celebration of the eucharist is the action of the whole Church" (International Commission on English in the Liturgy, *The Roman Missal*, page 19). Whereas a priest presides over the ritual of the Eucharist, the whole people, as a royal priesthood, share in the celebration by entering into the sacred mystery. The Mass is essentially a communal act.

◆ Recall the most meaningful celebration of the Eucharist that you have attended. What three characteristics made it this way?

◆ What are some characteristics of liturgies you have attended that held less meaning for you?

◆ Have you ever actually felt as if you shared in the royal priesthood at Mass? If so, how? If not, why not?

Ways to Be Involved

The congregation can actively participate in the Mass in a number of ways.

Listening

Active listening is essential for any relationship between persons who care about each other. In the Eucharist we have the opportunity not simply to hear words being pronounced but to listen with our whole self, expecting that God is trying to reach us. By actively listening to the readings and prayers, we attend not only to the person speaking but ultimately to God, who is the source of the Good News. During active listening we let our imagination form pictures of the biblical scenes, we apply the messages of the Scriptures to our situation, we make the words proclaimed our own.

Singing

"Those who sing pray twice" is an enduring old adage. Singing draws out our feelings in a way that simply reciting words cannot. A vast difference exists between saying the words of a great hymn like "Amazing Grace" and singing the hymn, because singing involves more of our whole self, and the beauty of the melody can reach our depths.

Singing also draws people together. A great moment at a major college football game is the singing of the fight song. Thousands of devoted fans—no matter how well they can carry a tune—stand up and belt out the lyrics and cheer madly after the last note. The song is a pledge of loyalty and a sign of unity. Songs at Mass usually have a gentler tone and quieter melody, but they serve the same purpose: they draw the group together and express the common beliefs and feelings of the community.

Reciting

At various points in the Mass, the assembly is called upon to recite prayers or responses. If the Gloria ("Glory to God in the highest . . .") is not sung, the congregation recites this ancient hymn of praise. After each petition of the Prayer of the Faithful, the community joins in by saying, "Lord, hear our prayer," or something similar. These responses can be recited mindfully or absentmindedly—with or without reflecting on their meaning. Mindful participation makes all the difference in the world because it consciously involves the people in the mystery they are celebrating.

Gesturing

Different postures and gestures have a place in praying the Mass. By consciously performing each posture or gesture, we signal our active participation. For instance, standing attentively to listen to the Gospel indicates our joy at receiving God's word. Before Communion, reaching over to give another person a sign of peace with a handshake or a hug shows our desire to be united and reconciled with everyone in the church and in our life.

Liturgical Ministry

Members of the community may participate in a special way in the Eucharist as readers (lectors), cross bearers, gift bearers, servers, musicians, or distributors of Communion (eucharistic ministers). Volunteering to help in one of these roles builds a person's sense of involvement in the celebration.

An Overview of the Ritual

As one of the sacraments of the church, the Eucharist is an occasion where we meet God and enter into God's life of grace in a special way. Before considering how we can participate most meaningfully in the different parts of this sacrament, let's look at the ritual as a whole.

The Names

Each of the two names usually used to designate the sacrament—Eucharist and Mass—points to something essential about it. The word *eucharist* comes from the Greek word that means "thanksgiving." Indeed the Eucharist is essentially a celebration of thanks for all God has done for us. It brings the life, death, and Resurrection of Jesus together with the life of everyone in the church as a sacrifice of praise and thanks to God.

The word *mass* comes from the final words of the Latin rite, *Ite missa est,* which mean "Go, you are dismissed (sent forth)." That is exactly what the Mass is intended to do—to direct us outward to be servants and healers and proclaimers of the Good News to the world. The Mass is for praising and thanking God, but it is also essentially for transforming us and moving us out into the world as the Body of Christ.

Sometimes the term *liturgy* is used to designate the Mass or the Eucharist. Recall that the liturgy is the official public prayer of the Catholic church. This is a broader category than just the Mass or the Eucharist. The liturgy includes all seven sacraments and the Divine Office. The word *liturgy* comes from the Greek word meaning "public service," which indeed is the worship of God by the community.

The Parts

The ritual of the Mass, or the Eucharist, is divided into two parts: the liturgy of the word and the liturgy of the Eucharist. This movement from word to Eucharist reflects the origins of the Mass in the Last Supper of Jesus with his disciples.

According to some Gospel accounts, the Last Supper was a Passover meal. This sacred Jewish feast, which happened once a year, celebrated the liberation of Israel from slavery in Egypt. Those gathered for the Passover always told the story of how God had freed the people from Pharaoh's rule, brought them miraculously through the sea, and made a Covenant with them. After the storytelling, they ate a sacrificial meal of unleavened bread and lamb. Wine was also a part of the ritual. The Passover meal incorporated the word or story of salvation, and the sharing of a sacrificial meal.

The Mass follows this same pattern. In the liturgy of the word, the community listens to the word of God, the story of how God has loved and saved the people. Then, in the liturgy of the Eucharist, the people eat a meal. The bread and wine served at this meal are not simply bread and wine; they are the body and blood of Christ, the Lamb of God. This meal celebrates the salvation of people from the slavery of sin and death, and the New Covenant God has made with us in Jesus. In the Mass the community is nourished by both word and Eucharist.

◆ How do stories nourish our spirit? Think of a story that has nourished you in some way.
◆ Reflect on a meal you have joined in where people shared stories and also themselves. How does that experience relate to what happens in the Eucharist?

The Rhythm

In the history of salvation, God initiates, and humans respond. God invites people to goodness and happiness and fullness of life, and they accept or reject the invitation.

The Mass follows this same rhythm. A word, a message, or a prayer is proclaimed, and the community responds. For example, after the presider offers certain prayers, the congregation says, "Amen." The lector proclaims the first reading from the word of God, and people then sing or say the responsorial psalm, so-called because it is a response to what has been proclaimed. Later the eucharistic prayer proclaimed by the priest leads to the response of the Great Amen sung by all those present.

This pattern of initiation and response can keep us mindful that God has first loved us and has given us Jesus Christ for our salvation. Our response is Eucharist—thanksgiving.

The Liturgy of the Word

The early Christian communities began their Sunday Eucharist by sharing the word. This ritual was patterned on the Scripture service that the Jews held every Sabbath in their synagogues. At first Christians shared only readings from the Hebrew Scriptures. But as the letters of Paul and other Apostles were written and passed around, and as the Gospels made their way into written form, these were added to the service of the word.

Over time the liturgy of the word developed several parts. Today at a Sunday Eucharist it consists of various introductory rites and of the proclamation of the word, which includes a profession of faith and the Prayer of the Faithful. Weekday Masses leave out some of these parts.

The Introductory Rites: Gathering Together

Liturgical celebrations should commence before the opening hymn or prayer. From the moment people arrive at church, they should feel welcomed. After all, they make up the Body of Christ. Each person should thus be received with the same hospitality that the community would extend to Jesus himself. Rather than avoiding one another, members of a community should greet one another and visit. Jesus constantly made it clear that hospitality is fundamental to charitable living. He ate with sinners and talked with outcasts. He mingled with anyone who would listen. Imagine what kind of accepting atmosphere that sort of hospitality would create in our churches!

Once people have entered the church and taken their seat, the introductory rites begin.

Entrance Procession and Greeting

As the priest, servers, and lector process into the church, the people stand and greet them, singing an entrance song. The song is intended to get the people into the spirit of worship and to generate a sense of unity and energy. A song sung by the whole community gives witness that the people are one in Christ, united in worshiping God. After the sign of the cross, the presider extends a greeting, setting a tone for the Mass and perhaps focusing people on its theme.

The Eucharist is meant to be celebrated in an atmosphere of hospitality.

Penitential Rite

The community confesses its sinfulness and asks, "Lord, have mercy." Sometimes it says the Confiteor ("I confess to almighty God") instead. During these moments of penitence, we might bring to mind times when we have slighted others or offered only cutting remarks, instances when we have walked by people in need, occasions of being dishonest with ourselves or others. These prayers for forgiveness attest to the reality that all people do wrong, but that God's grace is greater than sin. Mercy has come in Jesus.

Glory to God

The Gloria—an ancient hymn that gives praise and thanksgiving to God for simply being God—ideally is sung by the people. Then the priest offers the opening prayer, to which the people respond, "Amen." At this point the actual service of the word begins.

The Proclamation of the Word

Like the bread broken and shared in Communion, the word of God is meant to be "broken open" and shared as a source of nourishment during the Mass.

The word of God is proclaimed in typically three readings from the Scriptures. Each Sunday the same passages are read in all Catholic churches throughout the world. Many Protestant denominations use a similar set of readings each Sunday, and this is a sign of unity between Protestants and Catholics.

Three cycles of readings—called A, B, and C cycles—are covered in three years, so that much of the Bible is proclaimed and preached over a three-year period. The scriptural readings are meant not so much to give information as to convey the story of God's love for humankind and how we are to respond. They put into words the beliefs and faith of the Christian community.

First Reading and Responsorial Psalm

The first reading generally is from a book of the Hebrew Scriptures, and it relates to the theme of the Gospel reading. When the reading is finished, a period of reflective silence should follow, during which we try to realize what in the reading hit home for us. We can ask ourselves, How is God trying to touch me through this reading?

Then the congregation responds to the word with a psalm, preferably singing it. The responsorial psalm relates in meaning to the first reading or to the liturgical season.

Second Reading

The second reading is from the Christian Testament, usually from the Epistles of Paul or of another writer, but sometimes from the Acts of the Apostles or the Book of Revelation. This reading gives us an idea of how the early Christian communities received and lived their faith. Again, a period of silence after this reading provides a chance to reflect on how these words relate to our life.

Gospel Reading and Homily

Right before the Gospel reading, except during Lent, the congregation sings the Alleluia and a short verse. The word *alleluia,* which is synonymous with joy, roughly translated means "praise God!" We stand to show respect for the Good News and readiness to listen. In standing for the Gospel, we recognize with joy that Jesus the Savior is present and speaking to us.

Just before the Gospel reading, everyone traces a small cross on their forehead, lips, and heart to declare their willingness to keep an open mind and heart to God's word, and to proclaim that word in their life. Then the priest reads the Gospel.

The term *homily* comes from a Greek word meaning "conversation." In fact, records show that many early homilies were conversations between the presider and the community. Ideally, a homily following the Gospel will explain the readings, clarifying and interpreting their themes and meanings and showing how their messages apply to the lives of those present. We must listen actively to the readings and the homily if we are to find meaning in the Mass.

Another brief period of silent reflection follows the homily.

Profession of Faith

Professing their faith, usually by reciting the Nicene Creed, gives the congregation a chance to respond to the Good News by saying, in effect, "We have listened to the word and believe in the essential truth of that word."

Prayer of the Faithful

The liturgy of the word ends with petitions from the community that are called the Prayer of the Faithful. These petitions are either prepared ahead and read by a lector, or offered spontaneously by anyone in the assembly who has a concern. They focus on the immediate needs of the community and also on the needs of the whole church and the entire world, particularly those who are suffering. Petitions are offered for families who have lost a loved one, for people who are sick or dying, for victims of tragedies, for peace among warring groups or nations, for leaders of nations and the church, or for any other people and concerns.

◆ If you were composing the Prayer of the Faithful, what needs would you pray for?

The Liturgy of the Eucharist

Recall that the word *eucharist* means "thanksgiving." A spirit of thankfulness fills the prayers in the liturgy of the Eucharist. You may think of the most important part of the Mass as being the consecration of bread and wine into Jesus' body and blood, and certainly that is central. But the familiar words of consecration ("this is my body . . ."; "this is the cup of my blood . . .") are set within a long prayer that pours out thanks to God. Thanks are offered for all God's saving actions in our history as a people—most of all, for the gift of Jesus' life, death, and Resurrection. The liturgy of the Eucharist is the people's thankful response to receiving God's word, the Good News, in the first part of the Mass.

The liturgy of the Eucharist is both a communal meal and a sacrifice. As a meal it recalls the Last Supper and allows us to enter into the Eternal Supper in which Jesus shares himself with us as our spiritual food and drink. As a sacrifice it recalls the great sacrifice Jesus made in giving his life for us. More than that, it allows us to unite our own life and sufferings with Jesus' Passion and death. In this *we* become transformed into Jesus' body and blood, given for the life of the world. Moreover, if we are united with Jesus in his death, then we are united with him in his Resurrection. So Jesus' sacrifice is not just something in the past that we remember. It becomes one with our own experience and has the power to save us in the present.

The liturgy of the Eucharist has several parts: the preparation of the gifts, the eucharistic prayer, the Communion rite, and the concluding rite.

Preparation of the Gifts

Every meal requires preparation. For the eucharistic meal, the bread and wine need to be brought forward and presented. In the early centuries of the church, these staples of life were prepared in homes by members of the community. Although some parishes today use homemade unleavened bread, most are limited to using hosts. The ideal is that the bread actually look, feel, and taste like bread.

Carrying the bread and wine, members of the community process to the altar. Acting on behalf of the whole assembly, they hand these gifts over to the presider, who places them on the table or altar. Often other gifts from the community, like the donations to the collection, are also brought up. Many parishes, too, have reinstituted the ancient custom of bringing up food for poor people at this time. These groceries are later given to local food pantries or shelters.

The bread and wine symbolize the community's gift of itself to God.

The gifts offer witness that our possessions do not own us. The community offering says, in effect: "All good things come from the Creator. We give them back to God as a sign of our gratitude, and we share them with others to build up our community, the Body of Christ."

The early Christians were filled with a generous, grateful spirit that enabled them to share everything:

> All who believed were together and had all things in common; they would sell their possessions and goods and distribute the proceeds to all, as any had need. Day by day, as they spent much time together in the temple, they broke bread at home and ate their food with glad and generous hearts, praising God and having the goodwill of all the people. (Acts of the Apostles 2:44–47)

So the preparation of the gifts should be a festive act of giving thanks to God. The bread and wine serve as symbols of the community's gift of itself back to God, a gift that will be transformed into life for the whole world. The presider prays over the gifts, and the whole community asks God to accept them as a sacrifice.

◆ Think of something in your life that you could offer with the bread and wine during the Mass—some struggle or hardship, joy or hurt. Reflect on how that aspect of your life could be transformed into something life-giving for the world.

The Eucharistic Prayer

In the eucharistic prayer, God's promise of salvation is fulfilled again through God's action in the community. The presider makes the prayer on behalf of the community:

> We come to you . . .
>
> .   .   .   .
>
> We offer them . . .
>
> .   .   .   .
>
> We honor Mary . . .

It becomes each one's prayer when each person joins her or his heart and mind with that of the presider. Thus Jesus becomes present in the forms of bread and wine and in the community itself. The Covenant between God and God's people is renewed.

The text of the eucharistic prayer can vary from one celebration of the Mass to another, but all versions have the same basic elements.

The Preface

The eucharistic prayer starts with words of thanksgiving and praise that are called the preface. The text of the preface usually relates to the liturgical season or feast. At the end the community sings, "Holy, holy, holy . . ." (the joyous song of the angels recorded in Isaiah 6:3), and, "Hosanna. . . . Blessed is he who comes in the name of the Lord" (words that the crowd used at Jesus' triumphant entry into Jerusalem). The words of the preface capture the spirit of welcoming Christ the Messiah who comes in the Eucharist.

Calling Down of the Spirit

After the Holy, Holy, the priest calls on God to send the Holy Spirit to bless the gifts of bread and wine so that they may become the body and blood of Christ. Later the Spirit will be invoked to unite the people themselves and to fill them so that they may become "one body, one spirit in Christ." It is by God's power, not our own, that the gifts of bread and wine and our own life are to be transformed.

Consecration

At the heart of the eucharistic prayer is the account of the Last Supper, with Jesus' words of consecration of the bread and wine:

Take this, all of you, and eat it:
this is my body which will be given up for you.
Take this, all of you, and drink from it:
this is the cup of my blood,
the blood of the new and everlasting covenant.
It will be shed for you and for all
so that sins may be forgiven.
Do this in memory of me.

In response to the sacrificial act of Jesus, the people offer a prayer of faith called the memorial acclamation. Several options exist for this, the most familiar being "Christ has died, Christ is risen, Christ will come again." The congregation proclaims that this paschal mystery is at the center of their faith and is the source of their salvation.

Remembrance, Offering, and Intercessions

Following the consecration, the presider declares that remembering Christ's sacrifice of himself, the whole community offers that sacrifice to God for the salvation of the world. Prayers for the church, especially its leaders, and for those who have died draw the eucharistic prayer toward its ending. But first the assembly is reminded of its unity with all those who have gone before—Mary, the Apostles, the entire communion of saints. Christianity is a communal religion. So these prayers remind the congregation that this Eucharist is celebrated with and for all God's people, living and dead.

> **The assembly is reminded of its unity with all who have gone before.**

Great Amen

A doxology (prayer of praise) concludes the eucharistic prayer. The priest sings or says, "Through [Jesus], with him, in him, in the unity of the Holy Spirit, all glory and honor is yours, almighty Father, for ever and ever," and then the community sings or says a hearty, "Amen!"—signaling its approval of all that has just happened. This response is called the Great Amen.

Notice that the pattern of prayer followed in the liturgy of the word is maintained in the liturgy of the Eucharist: the action of God is proclaimed by the presider, and the community is invited to respond with praise and thanksgiving, faith and love.

◆ Recall an especially memorable meal that you had with family or friends. Remember how it started, what was said, who was there, the mood of everyone, and, in particular, what about your own attitude and actions made this meal special.

◆ Think of five living people who need your prayers, and at least one deceased person you would like to remember. Carry them in your heart to Mass and pray for them at the appropriate times in the eucharistic prayer.

◆ To sing or say "Amen" is like singing or saying a strong "Yes!" Jesus becomes present in the Eucharist in a special way, but he is present in other blessed events, too. When you go to Mass, think of one of those times and recall it as you say or sing "Amen" at the end of the eucharistic prayer.

Communion Rite

With the eucharistic prayer ended, the community readies itself to perform the Communion rite—to eat and drink the sacred meal.

The Lord's Prayer and the Sign of Peace

The people join in the Lord's Prayer, the prayer that Jesus taught us. The prayer reminds them that God gives daily bread (takes care of our practical needs), but also gives the body of Christ (takes care of our spiritual needs). The prayer also reminds the community that they need to forgive one another's faults in order to receive the Eucharist worthily.

The offering of a handshake or a hug at the sign of peace pulls people out of their small world to join with the whole church. Even if people do not know one another, or divisions split the community, this gesture challenges the assembly to value one another and to extend healing and harmony to one another. Think of the sign of peace as more than a chance to greet a neighbor in the pew in a friendly way. It is that, but much more. It is a sign of being one in Christ, and of exchanging not simply our own friendliness, but the deep peace of Christ. In addition, it reminds us of the need to share that peace with others outside of Mass.

Breaking of the Bread

At the Last Supper, Jesus took one loaf of bread, broke it, and distributed it to his disciples. Eating from the same loaf signaled that all were part of the same community. As Saint Paul said, in the Communion rite, "because there is one bread, we who are many are one body, for we all partake of the one bread" (1 Corinthians 10:17).

At this point in the Mass, the presider breaks the bread. The act of breaking the bread has stronger symbolism when a single loaf is divided to feed the community. Although most churches, for convenience, use hosts, each Communion station may be given a section broken from a large host to distribute. While the bread or host is being broken, the people sing or say the Lamb of God, asking for Christ's mercy and peace: "Lamb of God, you take away the sins of the world: / have mercy on us. . . ."

Communion

Before the priest and people receive Communion, or the body and blood of Christ as bread and wine, they join in saying a prayer of humility and openness to the power of what they are about to do: "Lord, I am not worthy to receive you, / but only say the word and I shall be healed."

While the people come forward to receive the body and blood of Christ, the community can sing together to celebrate and express that they are one body in Christ. Today, as in ancient times, people stand to receive the Eucharist—a sign of joy. They receive the bread in their hand and then reverently eat it. They are given the cup to hold and to drink from.

The communicants say, "Amen," when they receive the body and blood of Jesus. This attests not only to their acceptance of Jesus, but also to their oneness with everyone else in the Body of Christ.

When everyone has shared Communion, time is allowed for silent prayer or a reflective song.

◆ **Reflect on some of the things you might pray about in the time after Communion. This is an ideal time to thank God—for the love God pours out through your family, friends, neighbors; for the often ignored miracles of creation like newborn babies, dazzling sunsets, music, laughter, and your body, brain, skills, and talents. You might also reflect on your unity with others in the church or with those who are suffering throughout the world. You might ponder how you can become "bread," or Jesus, for some person who needs you.**

Concluding Rite

After the reflection period following Communion, brief announcements that deal with the life of the community or call people to service may be made. Then, to carry out the concluding rite—to bring the Mass to a close—the presider first blesses the assembly in the name of the Trinity. He dismisses the people, reminding them to leave in the peace of Christ. They are to go forth and spread the Good News, loving and serving God. They are to *be* Christ's heart, hands, and voice to a world that desperately needs love.

Keeping the Emmaus Experience with Us

Let's return to the story from Luke's Gospel that opened this chapter, the account of the disciples' sharing the Eucharist with Jesus on the road to Emmaus. After Jesus vanished from their sight, the disciples said to each other, "'Were not our hearts burning within us while he was talking to us on the road, while he was opening the scriptures to us?'" (Luke 24:32). Later, to the Apostles back in Jerusalem, the disciples "told what had happened on the road, and how [Jesus] had been made known to them in the breaking of the bread" (verse 35). They were describing what we have been calling the liturgy of the word and the liturgy of the Eucharist.

For these disciples the Eucharist was not a ritual. Rather, they experienced it as a powerful, mysterious, but very warm and human interaction with the Risen Jesus, an event that transformed them forever. As we contemporary Christians appreciate the ritual beauty of the Eucharist, let us also sense the power and freshness of the eucharistic experience that these disciples had so long ago on the road to Emmaus.

11

TRADITIONAL PRAYER

PRAYING TOGETHER IN ONE VOICE

A few decades ago, when Catholics heard the word *prayer,* they thought immediately of the traditional formulas they memorized as children: the Lord's Prayer, the Hail Mary, the Prayer of Praise, and so on. Catholics have since become accustomed to praying in more varied ways. But the tried-and-true traditional prayers still have great significance and value, as they have for millions of people over the centuries.

Why Traditional Prayers?

Perhaps the most important benefit of praying the traditional prayers of the church is that doing so unites us with a larger community of believers. It gives us the chance to pray with one voice.

In Union with the Church

Go anywhere in the world, and if you meet Christians, they will likely know and recite the Lord's Prayer—in their own language, but with the same meaning everywhere. Roman Catholics will commonly say the Hail Mary, the Apostles' Creed, the rosary, and other prayers that have become an important part of Catholic religious experience. Use of these prayers helps a Catholic to feel bonded to the worldwide Catholic Christian community.

A similar thing happens with a game like soccer. All over the world, millions of people play this international game, and the rules vary only slightly from place to place. Imagine two soccer players from Hungary visiting South Korea. They are out walking and observe a pickup game in progress. A ball rolls out of bounds, and one of the Hungarians kicks it precisely to one of the Korean players. The Koreans wave to the Hungarians to join them because the teams are short of players. Since the Koreans play soccer by the same rules, the game proceeds without a hitch. The Hungarians enjoy themselves and feel just a bit closer to the Koreans, and the Koreans show their hospitality and welcome to the foreign visitors. In short, certain standard practices link people together and give them a chance to belong to the larger community.

Think, too, of what happens at a sports game between schools when the fans of one school want to cheer on their team or send them a message from the stands. They all join their voices to call out one cheer; they do not send separate, individual messages to the team. A group cheer is unifying and powerful. It reaffirms for the fans who they are (their identity as a school) and what they stand for (their belief in their team and school).

National anthems function in a similar way, giving a unified expression to people's ideals about their country. And when we pray traditional Christian or Catholic prayers, we unite ourselves with other Christians or Catholics, reaffirming who we are as a people and what we believe. This is true even when we pray privately or silently. The traditional prayers themselves are a bond between us.

When Words Fail Us

Sometimes we need to lean on the wider community to supply us with words when it is just too hard for us to come up with our own prayers spontaneously. Like a valentine that offers just the right message to someone we care about when we can't find our own words, traditional prayers can serve us well. Here is an example from the news:

> A fisherman . . . lost and presumed drowned after being caught in a sudden squall in a small boat . . . was found after more than two days and rushed to a hospital. That's where a television reporter found him. . . .
>
> "Were you scared out there, all alone, cold, and wet?" asked the news reporter.
>
> "Yes," replied the seaman.
>
> The reporter had obviously hoped for something more . . . well, more viewer-friendly.
>
> "What did you do out there on the ocean during all those scary hours?" he persisted.
>
> "I prayed," said the seaman laconically.
>
> "Prayed?" responded the reporter. "What did you pray?"
>
> "Oh, you know. Your basic Our Father and Hail Mary." The seaman's elementary religiousness seemed to befuddle his more worldly interviewer, who did a quick wrap-up and closed out fast. (John Deedy, "How Do You Rate Your Prayer Life?" *U.S. Catholic,* May 1990, page 6)

The seaman's answer would not make flashy material for the nightly news, but his simple prayer clearly helped him get through this ordeal at sea. In times of trouble, creativity may come hard, so people turn to the tried-and-true. The Our Father (Lord's Prayer) and the Hail Mary connected the lost fisherman to a God whom he sought for comfort and rescue.

◆ What is your approach to traditional prayers? Do you find them appealing as a way to pray? Why or why not?

The Lord's Prayer: From the Heart of Jesus

For Christians, the most important traditional prayer is the Lord's Prayer, or the Our Father—the prayer Jesus taught his followers. Great theologians in the church's history have called it "the summary of the whole gospel" and the "most perfect of prayers" because it expresses so well what the Good News is all about (United States Catholic Conference, *Catechism of the Catholic Church,* number 2774).

The Gospels offer two versions of the Lord's Prayer. Luke's Gospel gives a short text (11:2–4), but we use the longer version found in Matthew's Gospel (6:9–13). In general practice and in the church's liturgy, archaic words like *thy* (for "your") and *art* (for "is") are retained because they are part of the familiar and beloved wording that most people grew up with. Here is the version most familiar to us as Jesus' model of how to pray:

> Our Father who art in heaven,
> hallowed be thy name.
> Thy kingdom come.
> Thy will be done on earth, as it is in heaven.
> Give us this day our daily bread,
> and forgive us our trespasses,
>   as we forgive those who trespass against us,
> and lead us not into temptation,
> but deliver us from evil.

The early Christians, when praying the Lord's Prayer in their liturgy, added to it a concluding line of praise, which is now included with the prayer at Mass:

> For the kingdom, the power and the glory are yours, now and forever.

Why is the Lord's Prayer so essential? Consider the context in which the prayer was given by Jesus to his followers. In Jesus' Middle Eastern culture, when people asked a religious teacher to show them how to pray, they were actually asking for a summary of the teacher's beliefs. Every religious group during Jesus' time had one prayer that contained the most important points of its teachings—a kind of creed for that group.

Thus when Jesus told his followers to pray using the words of the Lord's Prayer, he was, in effect, saying: "This is the essence of my belief. These words tell you how to talk with God." The Lord's Prayer shows people how to relate to God and live in right relation with other people. Because it remains the most complete statement of Jesus' prayer, it is prominent in the Mass and in all church rites.

Think of the Lord's Prayer as divided into two parts: the first part, "Our Father . . . as it is in heaven," draws us toward God's glory; the second part, "Give us this day . . . but deliver us from evil," expresses our concerns for ourselves in the world. The first part contains three petitions, and the second part has four. Let's take it phrase by phrase.

Our Father Who Art in Heaven

The Lord's Prayer begins by calling out to God as Father, naming the one we are praying to.

Jesus chose to begin with the plural *our* instead of the singular *my*. This *our* implies that we belong to one another—us to God, God to us, us to one another. By using the plural, Jesus was acknowledging that we need always to pray as a community, even when we pray in private. Christians never really pray alone because Jesus' followers always pray as part of the family of God. By claiming God as *our* Father, not simply *my* Father, Christians commit themselves to loving all women and men as sisters and brothers.

What about addressing God as Father? This was how Jesus related to God, whom he knew intimately as his loving parent. On another occasion Jesus used the Aramaic term *Abba,* which is better translated as "Dad," "Papa," "Daddy," or "Dearest Father." It signals a comfortably affectionate relationship between parent and child, not a formal, distant one.

◆ Say the Lord's Prayer, substituting *my* and *me* for *our* and *us*. How does this change feel to you?

If Jesus had lived in a different culture and a different time, he might have called on God as "our Mother." After all, God is not male or female, but simply God: the perfect and complete parent—father, mother, and much more. In Isaiah's prophecy God says, "'As a mother comforts her child, / so I will comfort you'" (66:13). The important point is that God comforts and loves, guides and protects us.

In addressing God as our Father "who art in heaven," we are not referring to God's living in a space beyond us. "In heaven" refers to a way of being, not a certain place. God dwells in the hearts of those who love, and having God live within us is heaven itself. As the Apostle John reminds us, "God is love, and those who abide in love abide in God, and God abides in them" (1 John 4:16). The love that we give and receive in our everyday human life is a glimpse of heaven.

Hallowed Be Thy Name

Once we have centered ourselves in God's presence with the opening of the Lord's Prayer, we move into the seven petitions. The first three petitions are concerned with drawing us toward God's glory. "Hallowed be *thy* name," *"thy* kingdom come," *"thy* will be done . . ." are petitions focused on God, not ourselves.

To ask that God's name be hallowed is to pray that God's name be recognized as holy. We say that God deserves to be praised and thanked for being wonderful and awesome, and that the whole world should glorify God. But we pray in particular that God's holiness might be known in the world through *our* actions, *our* life.

Thy Kingdom Come

Human beings are unique among the animals because they can imagine things that have not yet come to reality. Those who sincerely pray, "thy kingdom come," are stretching their imagination to dream of a world in which God's reign (kingdom) of justice, love, and peace will be a reality. They are dreaming about our world, not some remote pie-in-the-sky place. Like people trapped in the rubble of a collapsed building after an earthquake, they long for deliverance. They wait and wait, calling out for help, eager for sounds that rescue is on the way. When they hear a noise, they call out even louder, all the while imagining the moment when they will be freed and reunited with their loved ones. To pray, "thy kingdom come," is to recognize that God is the ultimate rescuer, coming to free us and the whole world. At the same time, this petition urges Christians to join with God in the rescue efforts.

The Kingdom of God, that reign of God's justice, love, and peace, is something we look toward and work toward for the future. But it is also already in our midst because Jesus has been given to us by God. The Kingdom is here, but not fully. We see the signs of the Kingdom every time we see love and compassion at work in the world, and we create the Kingdom with God by letting God's love and mercy flow through us. So "thy kingdom come" refers to our longings for God's Reign in the present as well as the future.

◆ In what ways do your own positive actions help build the Reign of God in the world?

Thy Will Be Done on Earth, as It Is in Heaven

When we pray that God's will be done, we are pledging ourselves to follow the example of Jesus, who summed up God's will when he said: "'I give you a new commandment, that you love one another. Just as I have loved you, you also should love one another'" (John 13:34). Jesus freely chose to do God's will, loving others, and so can we.

The phrase "on earth, as it is in heaven" reminds us that we are praying that God's will might be done in the entire world, not just in our own individual life. The reference to heaven again does not mean a particular place. We should not imagine that God's will is now being done someplace else, far away, and that we have to duplicate it here on earth. No, the idea is to turn the whole earth into heaven, that is, into the place where God dwells and reigns fully.

Give Us This Day Our Daily Bread

The plea "Give us this day our daily bread" begins the second part of the Lord's Prayer, the four petitions that focus on our own concerns and well-being.

This petition expresses the childlike trust and belief that all good things ultimately come from God. Even though we may have "earned" our bread—or any other material goods, like our house, clothes, car, and so on—we acknowledge that everything we have is a gift from God, something to be shared not hoarded. Furthermore, this prayer is for the needs of the whole human family: "Give *us*," not *"me."* It reminds us of our responsibility to all those who go without the material necessities of life. God's will—that justice be done for all people—cannot be accomplished apart from human beings, ourselves, taking action.

This petition also recalls for us the Bread of Life, the gift of God's word and of Jesus given to us in the Eucharist. By praying, "Give us this day our daily bread," we remember that physical hunger is only one of many types of hunger, that humanity is perishing for lack of spiritual nourishment, and that we are called to bring God's word and sacraments to a hungry world.

◆ Think of as many people as you can who give you your "daily bread." Say a prayer of thanksgiving for them.

And Forgive Us Our Trespasses, as We Forgive Those Who Trespass Against Us

All of us sin, that is, we harm our relationships with God and with other people. Thus, we stand in need of healing and forgiveness from God and our neighbors.

God will forgive us readily. Jesus made this clear in the parable of the lost sheep, in which a shepherd leaves his flock to go off in search of one sheep that is missing. He is overjoyed when he finds the lost sheep. Jesus explained that "'there will be more joy in heaven over one sinner who repents than over ninety-nine righteous persons who need no repentance'" (Luke 15:7). Forgiveness is there for the asking.

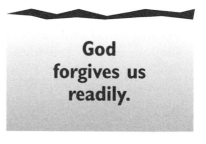

God forgives us readily.

God wants to keep the relationship with us open, no matter how we have failed.

But this petition involves more than asking God to forgive us our "trespasses" (our debts or offenses). The second part of the petition is indispensable to the first: "as we forgive those who trespass against us." This is not simply a nice afterthought. The point is that God's mercy and forgiveness cannot even reach us and touch us if our heart has been closed and hardened by refusing to forgive others who have "trespassed" against us.

◆ Think of a person you need to forgive for some wrong against you. Imagine yourself forgiving that person. Then think of something that needs forgiveness in you, and imagine God surrounding you with mercy for it.

And Lead Us Not into Temptation

The petition "and lead us not into temptation" does not imply that God actually tempts people to do evil. The opposite is true: God wants to set us free from evil. A better translation of the original Greek is, "and do not allow us to enter into temptation."

Temptation always appears as a good thing, promising us some form of happiness. That is why we are drawn to it. But its promise is an illusion, a lie. So in this petition, we ask God for the strength and wisdom to help us see this illusion for what it is and walk away from it. God will not take away our freedom to choose temptation, but God can help us discern true good from phony goods with the Spirit's help.

But Deliver Us from Evil

The final petition of the Lord's Prayer, "but deliver us from evil," implores God to do exactly what God is longing to do—save us from evil. By praying that prayer, we unite ourselves with God's longing, saying to God: "I want what you want. I want to be rescued from everything that could take me away from you." It is another way of saying, "Thy will be done."

Notice that the petition refers to *us*, not simply to *me*. We are praying for the whole human family when we offer this petition, placing all the world's distress and agony into God's hands and asking that God deliver the world from every evil that drags it down—war, famine, homelessness, poverty, injustice, hatred, greed, drug addiction, and so on.

The final words of the Lord's Prayer, "For the kingdom, the power and the glory are yours, now and forever," bring us back to a spirit of praising God. When we say "Amen" at the end, we are, in a way, underlining what we have just said, emphasizing it with a kind of exclamation, "So be it!"

As the universal cry of Christians taught by Jesus himself, the Lord's Prayer sums up the beliefs and aspirations of Christian faith about our relationship with God and one another.

◆ Now that you have considered its meaning, go back and pray the Lord's Prayer slowly and reflectively. What occurs to you that does not usually come to mind as you pray this prayer?

Prayers of Faith in the Trinity

The basic stance of Christian prayer is to address God our Creator through Jesus Christ, in union with the Holy Spirit. Even when prayer to God does not specifically mention the three persons of the Trinity, it is trinitarian in its approach to God simply because it is Christian.

Some prayers—like the Sign of the Cross, the Prayer of Praise, the Apostles' Creed, and Come Holy Spirit—refer specifically to the Trinity and remind us of the distinctly Christian understanding of God as Creator, Redeemer, and Sanctifier—Father, Son, and Holy Spirit.

The Sign of the Cross and the Prayer of Praise

The first prayer taught to most Catholic children when they are old enough to make a cross on themselves is the sign of the cross. It is the most common way that we acknowledge that we are people who belong to the Trinity and that we do everything in the name of the Trinity. The words are accompanied by the gesture of reverently making a cross with the right hand from one's forehead to heart to left shoulder to right shoulder.

The sign of the cross often opens and closes other, longer prayers, but it can be said anywhere at any time as a reminder that we belong to God and that the cross is our sign of salvation. The familiar prayer goes:

> **We belong to the Trinity and do everything in the name of the Trinity.**

> In the name of the Father,
> and of the Son,
> and of the Holy Spirit. Amen.

With a slight variation and an addition, the prayer becomes the Prayer of Praise, the traditional way to praise God as Trinity and to recall that God is in all of life—past, present, and future:

> Glory to the Father,
> and to the Son,
> and to the Holy Spirit:
> as it was in the beginning, is now, and will be for ever.
> Amen.

The Apostles' Creed

Another major prayer of Christian tradition comes to us from the early church and is still widely used today. Called the Apostles' Creed, it summarizes the beliefs of the Christian faith as handed down to the early Christian communities by the Apostles. The creed recited at Mass, the Nicene Creed, is a later statement of belief that is longer and has more philosophical language.

Based on belief in the three persons of the Trinity, the Apostles' Creed was part of the initiation of new Christians, who memorized the prayer and professed it as a requirement for baptism:

> I believe in God, the Father almighty,
>   creator of heaven and earth.

> I believe in Jesus Christ, his only Son, our Lord.
>   He was conceived by the power of the Holy Spirit
>   and born of the Virgin Mary.
>   He suffered under Pontius Pilate,
>   was crucified, died, and was buried.

He descended to the dead.
On the third day he rose again.
He ascended into heaven, and is seated at the right
    hand of the Father.
He will come again to judge the living and the
    dead.

I believe in the Holy Spirit,
    the holy catholic Church,
    the communion of saints,
    the forgiveness of sins,
    the resurrection of the body,
    and the life everlasting.

Come Holy Spirit

Praying directly to God as Father and God as Jesus Christ seems to come fairly easily. The Holy Spirit, however, is less often prayed to—and perhaps forgotten. Jesus sent the Spirit to us to be our Advocate and Counselor. The Holy Spirit inspires and moves people all over the world in ways we do not expect. The Holy Spirit deserves special, direct prayer from us. The most well known prayer to the Spirit is Come Holy Spirit:

Come, Holy Spirit, fill the hearts of your faithful
    and kindle in them the fire of your love.

Send forth your Spirit, and they shall be created:
    And you will renew the face of the earth.

With these words, Christians invite the always present Spirit into their heart. The Spirit sets hearts on fire with love, which dispels darkness and despair. With this love, God's people can be moved to "renew the face of the earth"—make peace, serve one another, act justly, heal the sick, and relieve suffering. Jesus sent the Spirit into the hearts of the faithful so that Jesus' presence would be felt on earth as it was during his actual lifetime. The Spirit is felt whenever and wherever the church acts as Jesus would.

◆ Think of a situation in which it would be particularly important to call on the Holy Spirit.

Prayers to and with Mary

As companions in the struggle to seek God and do God's will, the saints, living and dead, form a powerful union of hearts and minds all pulling toward the good. Those who have gone before us in death are particularly close to God, and by praying with them, we grow closer to God through them.

First among the saints is Mary, the mother of Jesus. Over the two thousand years of Christianity, Mary has always played a special role in the lives of believers. She is the saint to whom Christians have turned when they have been most in distress, most in need of healing. At times over the centuries, popular piety was so full of Marian devotion that people rarely prayed directly to God, no doubt because their image of God was mistakenly that of a remote, majestic being who could not possibly be involved with them. Mary, on the other hand, seemed close, accessible, and warmly interested in them.

The Hail Mary

Jesus' mother, Mary, has taken on the role of being mother of all of us. The special prayer to Mary familiar to Catholics is the Hail Mary (in Latin, Ave Maria). The prayer has two parts: one part praises God for all the good God has done through Mary, and the other entrusts our needs and prayers, even at the time of our death, into Mary's hands to take to God. Here is the ancient, beloved prayer:

> Hail, Mary, full of grace, the Lord is with you.
> Blessed are you among women,
> and blessed is the fruit of your womb, Jesus.
> Holy Mary, Mother of God, pray for us sinners,
>   now and at the hour of our death.
> Amen.

In its first part, the prayer recalls the Annunciation, the visit of the angel Gabriel to Mary, during which the angel greets her and announces that God is with her, blessing her with a coming child who will be the long-awaited Messiah (Luke 1:26–38). It also recalls the story of the Visitation, Mary's visit to her cousin Elizabeth. The older woman, also pregnant with a son, greets Mary with praise for what God has created in her, declaring the child in Mary's womb "blessed" (Luke 1:39–45).

The second part of the Hail Mary, beginning with "Holy Mary," calls upon Mary as Mother of God to care for us too—to act as our mother as well as Jesus' mother. By acknowledging that we are sinners, we tell Mary how needy we are, how much we require mercy and compassion. We ask her to be with us today and all the way to the end of our life—just as she was with Jesus at his death on the cross. We look to her to guide us into the arms of God.

The Hail Mary is a prayer of great joy and trust.

The Magnificat

A beautiful, strong prayer in the Christian tradition comes from the same chapter in the Gospel of Luke that tells the story of the Annunciation and the Visitation. This prayer is Mary's out-pouring of praise to God for all God's blessings, in her and in all generations. She is filled with joy when Elizabeth greets her as "the mother of my Lord." This prayer, which we know as the Magnificat, flows from Mary's whole being:

> My soul magnifies the Lord,
>> and my spirit rejoices in God my Savior,
> for he has looked with favor on the lowliness of his
>> servant.
>> Surely, from now on all generations will call me
>> blessed;
> for the Mighty One has done great things for me,
>> and holy is his name.
> His mercy is for those who fear him
>> from generation to generation.
> He has shown strength with his arm;
>> he has scattered the proud in the thoughts of their
>> hearts.
> He has brought down the powerful from their thrones,
>> and lifted up the lowly;
> he has filled the hungry with good things,
>> and sent the rich away empty.

He has helped his servant Israel,
>   in remembrance of his mercy,
according to the promise he made to our ancestors,
>   to Abraham and to his descendants forever.

(Luke 1:46–55)

Mary's song of praise reflects a woman alive with a passion for justice and mercy. She believes in a God who is on the side of people who are poor, hungry, abused, oppressed. In stark contrast to some images of her as meek, mild, and subservient, the woman revealed in this prayer has great strength and conviction. She is aware that God is doing extraordinary things for all generations through her cooperation.

The Magnificat is a song of praise to God, but it also calls Christians to let God work through them—as God did through Mary—to feed those who are hungry, free people from oppression, and challenge systems that are unjust. Mary's prayer summarizes what Jesus himself would stand for in his own life and ministry.

◆ **What images do you have of Mary? If she were alive today on earth, what might she be doing with her life?**

The Rosary

Many legends surround the origins of the prayer we call the rosary. The term *rosary* originally meant "rose garden." One ancient legend had it that a young man was praying the Hail Mary over and over again, and Mary appeared to him. As he said each Hail Mary, she turned the prayer into a rosebud, which she later wove into a crown. Another story attributes the rosary to an encounter of Saint Dominic with the Blessed Mother.

What is known is that the rosary has been a fixed part of Catholic devotion since the Middle Ages, as a kind of substitute for the liturgy of the hours. It was officially approved by the pope in the 1500s. Regardless of its origins, the rosary attracted people centuries ago because it was a simple prayer, learned easily. Because the vast majority of people in the Middle Ages could not read, they could not pray the Psalms or certainly the complicated Divine Office, or liturgy of the hours, which included the Psalms. Simple, uneducated people loved Mary, the mother of Jesus. So they developed the custom of saying 150 Hail Marys (instead of the 150 Psalms), and usually just the first part of each Hail Mary.

Gradually the praying of the Hail Marys became ritualized into the format of decades that we are familiar with today (a decade consists of an Our Father, ten Hail Marys, and the Prayer of Praise). Typically, rosary beads are used to keep count. Before praying the decades (either five decades for a short rosary or fifteen for the full rosary), we begin with these prayers:
1. The Sign of the Cross
2. The Apostles' Creed
3. Three Hail Marys
4. The Prayer of Praise

After all the decades (five or fifteen) have been said, the rosary closes with another ancient prayer to Mary, Hail Holy Queen:

> Hail, holy Queen, mother of mercy,
> Our life, our sweetness, and our hope.
> To you do we cry,
> poor banished children of Eve.
> To you do we send up our sighs,
> mourning and weeping in this vale of tears.
> Turn then, most gracious advocate,
> your eyes of mercy toward us,
> and after this exile
> show to us the blessed fruit of your womb, Jesus.
> O clement, O loving,
> O sweet Virgin Mary.

For many people, reciting the rosary is a way of focusing their attention on the presence of God and clearing out the clutter of worries and activities. Many other religions have similar repetitious prayer forms: for instance, Muslims and Buddhists use prayer beads. Such repetitious prayer can create a contemplative awareness of God, forming a kind of background music for pondering the mysteries of faith.

In fact, probably the most well known way of praying the rosary is to use it as a background prayer for meditating on the various mysteries of Jesus' life, death, and Resurrection. Each decade is the occasion for meditating on a separate mystery, of which there are fifteen altogether: five joyful mysteries, five sorrowful mysteries, and five glorious mysteries. If we are saying a short rosary, we focus on one group of five mysteries. The mysteries are based on accounts from the Scriptures.

The Joyful Mysteries
1. Annunciation (Luke 1:26–38)
2. Visitation (Luke 1:39–56)
3. Nativity of Jesus (Luke 2:1–7)
4. Presentation of Jesus in the Temple (Luke 2:22–32)
5. Finding of the Child Jesus in the Temple (Luke 2:41–52)

The Sorrowful Mysteries
1. Agony in the Garden (Mark 14:32–36)
2. Scourging of Jesus (John 18:28–38; 19:1)
3. Crowning with Thorns (John 19:2–6)
4. Carrying of the Cross (John 19:12–16)
5. Crucifixion and Death of Jesus (Luke 23:33–34,39–46)

The Glorious Mysteries
1. Resurrection of Jesus (Luke 24:1–6)
2. Ascension of Jesus (Luke 24:50–53)
3. Descent of the Holy Spirit at Pentecost (Acts of the Apostles 2:1–4)
4. Assumption of Mary (Song of Songs 2:8–14)
5. Coronation of Mary as Queen of Heaven (Revelation 12:1–6)

A person praying the rosary need not feel constrained to meditate only on the prescribed mysteries of Jesus' life. For instance, if a person felt the need for reconciliation, he or she might meditate on the mystery of the Last Supper and the gift of God's mercy in the Eucharist.

◆ Which mystery of the rosary means the most for you to meditate on at this point in your life?

One Mind and Heart, One Voice

Christians have found comfort and inspiration in many traditional prayers. These prayers serve as a common language for Christians and Catholics, a way of expressing the beliefs that we hold together and of communicating with God when our own words fail us. Besides uniting us with God, these prayers then bond us in mind and heart to other members of the church, both living and dead, who have prayed these words, dreamed these dreams, voiced these longings.

EPILOGUE

GROWING IN A
LIFE OF PRAYER

The end of a book on prayer is a good opportunity to reflect on where you are with prayer and what difference it may be making in your life.

Looking Back on Your Experiences

Take some time to review what you have read in this book.

◆ Think over the prayer styles you have learned about and practiced. Go back over the chapter topics to help you remember. Do any of the prayer exercises you did strike you as especially helpful or fruitful? What seemed to be most in tune with you?

◆ Think back on your overall experience with prayer since you started the book. Have you been able to pray? In what ways have you changed or grown in prayerfulness? Have you noticed anything different in your attitudes or approaches to life? Were you expecting something in your heart or mind that did not happen? What did you learn about yourself and your inner being?

While reading this book, you have likely spent considerable time and energy getting in touch with prayer generally and learning specific ways of praying. No doubt you have been drawn to some methods of prayer more than to others, and that is not surprising. Your prayer, after all, is an expression of who you are, and everyone is unique.

It may be, too, that you have found yourself unable to pray in any of the ways described in this book. Or perhaps you tried praying but did not keep it up. If either of these is the case, try looking back over chapters 1 and 2, which give a broad notion of what it means to find God in your life and in the world. You may discover that you have actually been praying but have not recognized what you are doing as prayer.

Praying the Way We Can

As we try to grow in prayerfulness, we need to keep in mind that the usual way we grow is not by leaps and bounds but steadily and slowly. We need to cultivate patience toward ourselves and trust that God is doing something within us even when we cannot feel anything remarkable going on. It is more significant that we try to pray than that we have extraordinary or mystical experiences.

One well-loved saint is Thérèse of Lisieux, a Carmelite nun who lived about a hundred years ago in France and died at the young age of twenty-four. Thérèse had a simple, honest approach to prayer, uncomplicated by any attempts to make something extraordinary happen. Actually, for long periods of her life, she felt little or no consolation from praying. Still she kept on, believing that God was nourishing her in ways she did not know, even if she did not immediately experience that sustenance. She is now considered a great writer on the spiritual life, and her autobiography has become a spiritual classic.

Thérèse's advice was to pray in whatever way we can, not to be taken with some lofty image of prayer that does not seem true to who we really are. She never became proficient in the usual techniques of prayer taught in her day. Instead, about her own prayer life she said:

> I just do what children have to do before they've learnt to read; I tell God what I want quite simply, without any splendid turns of phrase, and somehow he always manages to understand me. For me, prayer means launching out of the heart towards God; it means lifting up one's eyes, quite simply, to heaven, a cry of grateful love, from the crest of joy or the trough of despair; it's a vast, supernatural force which opens out my heart, and binds me close to Jesus. (*Autobiography of St. Thérèse of Lisieux*, page 289)

In Thérèse's understanding, prayer is a movement of the heart to God, whether the heart is joyful or despairing. She believed we should simply gather up our everyday experiences, good and bad, and lift them up to God—even if we do not see immediate results. This poem by a young woman from New Mexico offers a similar message:

In prayer, we can lift up our everyday experiences to God.

Jesus,
When I walk alone,
   I talk to myself,
     knowing that you are listening to me.
I talk to you,
   telling you my problems.
I tell you about my day
   and what it was like.
I ask if you are listening.
There is no answer.
I talk some more,
   telling you more,
     but still there is no answer from you.

Then when I feel free
> from all my problems and thoughts,
> I know that you, Jesus, were there for me.
> (Leontine Earl, in Carl Koch, editor, *Dreams Alive*, page 63)

Allowing Prayer to Change Us

How do we know that our prayer is genuine? How do we know that we are getting anywhere at all with prayer?

When we genuinely pray, no matter what method we use, we are opening our heart and our life to God and letting God work within us. A helpful saying is this: "Prayer doesn't change things. Prayer changes people, and people change things."

How do we know that we are actually changing, and in what way can we expect prayer to change us? Jesus tells us: "'Every good tree bears good fruit. . . . You will know [the trees] by their fruits'" (Matthew 7:17–20). If we are praying from the heart, eventually we will see the changes prayer makes in our life. Those fruits will appear not necessarily while we are praying or soon after we begin a habit of prayer, but gradually over time. The fruits of prayer can be seen in growth in the life of God within a person—growth in the virtues of faith, hope, and love.

Growing in faith. Faith is belief in God but also trust, a willingness to put ourselves in God's hands because we know that God is with us and for us, caring for us every moment. Faith leads to serenity and peace even in the midst of troubles and chaos.

◆ Have you noticed any movement in yourself toward trusting God more since you began reading this book on prayer?
◆ Bring to mind recent situations that seemed threatening, painful, or overwhelming to you. Did you respond to these troubles any differently than you used to?
◆ Which one of these statements characterizes you best: "I want God to be in my hands" or "I want to be in God's hands"?

Growing in hope. Hope is not the same as optimism, not simply a cheerful or positive outlook. Optimism tries to find reasons to think things are going to turn out right. Hope, on the other hand, sees possibilities even in apparently hopeless situations. It is the deep conviction that God is bringing forth good out of even the most desperate circumstances. This is the spirit of joy, courage, and righteous anger at injustice.

When we are hopeful, we look for God's action in the world and see it where others might not; we find good in people whom others have written off. Even more, hope moves us to join in bringing about the reign of God's justice, mercy, and peace, because we know that eventually, in the long run, God's goodness will triumph over all the evil in the world.

◆ Since you began studying this book, are you more apt to see things that you would characterize as God's action for good in the world?

◆ Have you found good qualities in people who others think are losers?

◆ Do you generally have a positive outlook? If so, is it because you have optimism, or because you have hope?

◆ Have you at times experienced joy, courage, or righteous anger?

Growing in love. Growing in love means more than having a bigger heart, although it can mean that too. When we are transformed by love, we are so filled with the love that is God that this love flows out to all those around us. We become a source of God's love for others as we develop the capacity for ever deepening relationships. Genuine prayer leads to giving ourselves to others and the world generously and joyfully. That is perhaps the most telling sign that we are growing in the spiritual life.

◆ Have you ever experienced love as filling you up so that it seems to flow right out of you to others?

◆ Have your relationships with others changed as you have learned how to live a prayerful life? If so, how?

◆ Have you been giving of yourself to others? If so, in what ways? Do you seem to be more giving than you used to be?

Growing Slowly and Well

We all need to realize that most people grow in faith, hope, and love at a very slow rate. We may be frustrated with our lack of "progress," figuring that if we did not make great strides while reading this book, we do not have a lot of potential in the spiritual life. But we need not become discouraged. God looks not for great leaps of faith, hope, and love from us, but for small efforts that bear fruit over time.

The prayer "Slow Me Down Lord," by Wilfred A. Peterson, gives a sense of what it means to grow in God's life, with patience and the belief that something marvelous is happening even when it is not obvious to us:

Slow me down, Lord! Slow me down!
Ease the pounding of my heart
by the quieting of my mind.

Steady my hurried pace
with a vision of the eternal reach of time.
Give me amid the confusions of my day,
the calmness of the everlasting hills.

Let me look upward
into the branches of the flowering oak
and know that it grew great
and strong
because it grew slowly and well.

Slow me down, Lord,
and inspire me to send my roots deep
into the soil
of life's enduring values
that I may grow
toward the stars
of my greater destiny.

Acknowledgments (continued)

The scriptural quotations contained herein are from the New Revised Standard Version of the Bible. Copyright © 1989 by the Division of Christian Education of the National Council of the Churches of Christ in the United States of America. All rights reserved.

The extract about Rosie on pages 10–11 is from "Rosie," in *Only the Heart Knows How to Find Them: Precious Memories for a Faithless Time,* by Christopher de Vinck (New York: Viking, 1991), pages 58–60. Copyright © 1991 by Christopher de Vinck. Used by permission of Viking Penguin, a division of Penguin Books USA.

The story of Andy on page 11 is from "Andy's Diner," by Jeff Behrens, in *Of Human Hands: A Reader in the Spirituality of Work,* edited by Gregory F. Augustine Pierce (Minneapolis: Augsburg Fortress; and Chicago: ACTA Publications, 1991), page 32. Copyright © 1991 by Augsburg Fortress. Reprinted by permission.

The quotes on page 19 describing what it means to pray, the extract on page 70 explaining what happens when we wake up to gratefulness, and the quote on pages 73–74 illustrating the joy of African children are from *Gratefulness, the Heart of Prayer: An Approach to Life in Fullness,* by David Steindl-Rast (New York and Ramsey, NJ: Paulist Press, 1984), pages 211, 11–12, and 18, respectively. Copyright © 1984 by David Steindl-Rast. Used by permission of Paulist Press.

The tale of the devout religious man on page 51 is from *Taking Flight: A Book of Story Meditations,* by Anthony de Mello (New York: Doubleday, 1988), pages 103–104. Copyright © 1988 by the Center for Spiritual Exchange. Used by permission of Doubleday, a division of Bantam Doubleday Dell Publishing Group.

The meditation steps on page 53 are quoted from *Praying with John Baptist de La Salle,* by Carl Koch (Winona, MN: Saint Mary's Press, 1990), page 51. Copyright © 1990 by Saint Mary's Press. All rights reserved.

The story of Joe on pages 59–609 is from "A Supportive Community," by Carol Luebering, in "The Communion of Saints: 'People Who Need People,'" by Leonard Foley, *Catholic Update* CU 1187, November 1987. Used by permission.

The story of the little fish on page 64 is from *The Song of the Bird,* by Anthony de Mello (Garden City, NY: Doubleday and Company, Image Books, 1984), page 12. Copyright © 1982 by Anthony de Mello. Used by permission of Doubleday, a division of Bantam Doubleday Dell Publishing Group.

Desmond Tutu's description of an experience in Mogopa, South Africa, on page 72, is from "Deeper into God," by Desmond Tutu, in

Cloud of Witnesses, edited by Jim Wallis and Joyce Hollyday (Mary-knoll, NY: Orbis Books, 1991), page 77. Copyright © 1991 by So-journers magazine and Orbis Books. Used by permission.

The writings quoted on pages 74 and 78 are from *Anne Frank: The Diary of a Young Girl,* translated by B. M. Mooyaart-Doubleday (New York: Random House, Modern Library, 1952), pages 184 and 12. Copyright © 1952 by Otto H. Frank. Used by permission of Double-day, a division of Bantam Doubleday Dell Publishing Group.

The insights of Edward Albee, James Baldwin, Robert Frost, and Adrienne Rich on pages 78–79 are quoted from *Research on Compos-ing: Points of Departure,* edited by Charles R. Cooper and Lee Odell (Urbana, IL: National Council of Teachers of English, 1978), pages 101–103. Copyright © 1978 by the National Council of Teachers of En-glish.

The extract on page 80 is from *Praying Our Experiences,* by Joseph F. Schmidt (Winona, MN: Saint Mary's Press, 1989), pages 7–8. Copyright © 1980, 1989 by Saint Mary's Press. All rights reserved.

The extract on page 81 is from *The Collected Works of St. Teresa of Ávila,* volume 2, translated by Otilio Rodriguez and Kieran Ka-vanaugh (Washington, DC: ICS Publications, 1980), page 284. Copy-right © 1980 by the Washington Province of Discalced Carmelites, ICS Publications, 2131 Lincoln Road NE, Washington, DC 20002.

The extract on page 91 is from *Letters to a Young Poet,* revised edition, by Rainer Maria Rilke, translated by M. D. Herter Norton (New York: W. W. Norton and Company, 1954), page 35. Copyright © 1954 by W. W. Norton and Company.

The poem by Anita Wheatcroft on page 93 and the story by Karen DeFilippis on pages 94–95 are from *Womenpsalms,* edited by Carl Koch (Winona, MN: Saint Mary's Press, 1992), pages 67 and 98–99. Copyright © 1992 by Saint Mary's Press. All rights reserved.

The words of Jon Kabat-Zinn on page 97 are quoted from an in-terview reproduced in *Healing and the Mind,* by Bill Moyers, edited by Betty Sue Flowers and David Grubin (New York: Doubleday, 1993), page 117. Copyright © 1993 by Public Affairs Television and David Grubin Productions. Used by permission of Doubleday, a divi-sion of Bantam Doubleday Dell Publishing Group.

The synopsis of Tolstoy's tale of a king searching for the answer to three questions, on pages 98–99, is from *On Being Present Where You Are: The James Backhouse Lecture, 1967,* Pendle Hill Pamphlet 151, by Douglas V. Steere (no place: Pendle Hill in association with Australia Yearly Meeting, 1967), pages 12–13. Copyright © January 1967 by Pendle Hill.

The extract on page 182 and the first excerpt on the back cover are from *Autobiography of St. Thérèse of Lisieux,* translated by Ronald Knox (New York: P. J. Kenedy and Sons, 1958), page 289, as quoted in *Praying with Thérèse of Lisieux,* by Joseph F. Schmidt (Winona, MN: Saint Mary's Press, 1992), page 80. Copyright © 1992 by Saint Mary's Press. All rights reserved.

The prayer by Leontine Earl on pages 182–183 is from *Dreams Alive: Prayers by Teenagers,* edited by Carl Koch (Winona, MN: Saint Mary's Press, 1991), page 63. Copyright © 1991 by Saint Mary's Press. All rights reserved.

The second excerpt on the back cover is from *The Hidden Ground of Love: The Letters of Thomas Merton on Religious Experience and Social Concerns,* selected and edited by William H. Shannon (New York: Farrar, Straus, Giroux, 1985), page 63. Copyright © 1985 by the Merton Legacy Trust.

The final excerpt on the back cover by Catherine McAuley is from *Prot. N. 1296: Dublin Documentary Study: Catherine McAuley,* volume 1 (Rome, 1985), page 782. Copyright © 1985 by M. Angela Bolster. Used with permission of the Sisters of Mercy, Dublin, Ireland.